Praise for Kidnapped Democracy

'Ramón Feenstra takes seriously the kidnap analogy as a conceptual tool with which to dissect the predicament of present-day democracies, engaging provocatively and meticulously with the identity, interests and strategies of both kidnappers and hostages, and the complex relationship between them, which culminates in a predictable and dramatic Stockholm syndrome. For how long will we be complacent, and will we justify the kidnap of our democracies and our lack of say in what happens to us?'
—**Sonia Alonso Saenz De Oger**,
Associate Professor of Government,
Georgetown University School of Foreign Service, Qatar

'This is a wonderful book. Kidnapping is a very strong metaphor to understand the democratic deficits of our time. Moreover, this is the right self-help book for victimized citizens to overcome their Stockholm syndrome and to develop democratizing practices'.
—**Paul Dekker**, Professor of Civil Society,
Tilburg University, The Netherlands

'To understand the challenges contemporary democracies face and to explore potential solutions addressing redemocratization, Feenstra uses the metaphor of kidnapping. The result is a very timely and provocative reflection looking at the present and to the future. A must read and discuss'.

—**Yanina Welp**,
Senior Researcher, Center for Democracy Studies;
Co-Director of the Zurich Latin American Center,
University of Zurich, Switzerland

KIDNAPPED DEMOCRACY

Polemics

Series Editors: Mark Devenney and Clare Woodford

Polemics draws on radical political philosophy and theory to address directly the various crises that have plagued global society and capitalism in the past decade. The series presents radical critiques of and alternative visions to the existing way of doing things. The texts in this series represent philosophically rigorous but polemical interventions in contemporary global, financial, political, environmental and theoretical crises. The series is published in partnership with CAPPE, University of Brighton.

Titles in the Series:

Kidnapped Democracy, by Ramón A. Feenstra

Against Free Speech, by Anthony Leaker

KIDNAPPED DEMOCRACY

Ramón A. Feenstra

ROWMAN & LITTLEFIELD
INTERNATIONAL

London • New York

Published by Rowman & Littlefield International, Ltd.
6 Tinworth Street, London SE11 5AL
www.rowmaninternational.com

Rowman & Littlefield International, Ltd. is an affiliate of
Rowman & Littlefield
4501 Forbes Boulevard, Suite 200, Lanham, Maryland 20706, USA
With additional offices in Boulder, New York, Toronto (Canada), and
London (UK)
www.rowman.com

British Library Cataloguing in Publication Information
A catalogue record for this book is available from the British Library

HB 978-1-78661-362-2
PB 978-1-78661-361-5

Library of Congress Cataloging-in-Publication Data Available

ISBN: 978-1-78661-362-2 (cloth : alk. paper)
ISBN: 978-1-78661-361-5 (pbk. : alk. paper)
ISBN: 978-1-78661-363-9 (electronic)

∞™ The paper used in this publication meets the minimum requirements of American National Standard for Information Sciences Perma-
nence of Paper for Printed Library Materials, ANSI/NISO Z39.48-1992.

CONTENTS

INTRODUCTION

Representative democracy and its basic structures have been kidnapped, at least in part. This is the idea that I will argue in this short book, the purpose of which is to provoke reflection on the current situation of the world's most widespread political system. Democracy has entered a complex and tumultuous period, and one of its main features – representation – is starting to show clear signs of weakness, urging a reassessment of its current state and its immediate future. Despite the obvious and nuanced differences between the kidnapping of individuals and the hijacking of political institutions that we must recognize, I will try to show how kidnappers, hostages and other victims can be identified in both situations, and how the hostages' freedom to act is thwarted by the repressive power of the kidnappers. I will also explain how both kidnapped and hijacked victims can suffer from Stockholm syndrome or rebel against their captors. The convergence of these two elements is what convinces me that this metaphor is especially suitable for reflecting on present-day democracy and on Western democratic systems (the focus of this short volume) in particular. This book progressively unpacks the various elements that expose the roles played by governments, political parties, the media, trade unions and a number of economic actors.[1]

---

1.   This book was inspired by the debates and discussions that surfaced during 'The Festival of Democracy' at the University of Sydney, September 2017. In addition, many of the reflections gathered here are indebted to the long conversations held since 2008 with Professor John Keane, to whom this book is dedicated.

I

RAISING THE ALARM

The United Nations Office on Drugs and Crime published its *Counter-Kidnapping Manual* in 2006 (UNDOC 2006), seeking to prevent this crime and mitigate its possible consequences. The manual contains a series of best practices and strategies for negotiators, police officers and authorities in general to respond as effectively and efficiently as possible. According to this report, a key first step is the initial detection of the event – the reporting of the kidnapping is obviously crucial here. In this regard, the UN manual indicates that alerts about 'an alleged kidnapping may reach the authorities in many different ways' but that usually 'it is a member of the family who, through a third party or a witness, reports the kidnapping by telephone to authorities or in person to a police officer'. That is, it is generally the kidnappers themselves who, after a few hours, contact the victims' relatives to state their demands, and the relatives then alert the authorities.

However, in the particular case we are dealing with, the kidnappers (intentionally) remain silent. This complicates both detection of the crime and identification of the captors, their demands and their motivations. In recent years, the kidnapping of democracy has subtly and steadily strengthened in numerous political contexts; this is not an issue that appears in news reports, at least for now. We live in an apparently calm period of established democracies, at least from a formal perspective (an aspect that should not be underestimated). The hijacking of democracy does not provoke the same outcry that is heard in other types of kidnappings, as we discuss below. In this case, we are not told what ransom the kidnappers demand for the safe return of their hostages since their only aim is to prolong and conceal the situation.

However, despite this initial constraint, a growing number of voices around the world are beginning to sound the alarm and accuse certain powerful forces of holding our democracy and its institutions hostage. These voices are diverse; however, they all concur in proclaiming the urgent need to restore freedom of action for representative institutions and citizenry. Until now, this warning has perhaps been ignored.

WRITERS, ACTIVISTS AND JOURNALISTS: THE FIRST TO SOUND THE ALARM

The warnings about the kidnapping of democracy are diverse and come from different sources.[1] During the presentation of his 2004 novel *Seeing* (*Ensayo sobre la Lucidez*, literally, 'Essay on Lucidity'), author Jose Saramago vividly expressed his concern. The novel's plot (I will not give too much away) reflects on the level of irrationality that political decisions can reach when a majority of the citizens of an important capital city decide to turn their backs on the political parties and cast blank ballots, to the complete bewilderment of the ruling classes. Saramago expressed his disquiet about how politics has gone astray both in the novel and in presentations of the book in Barcelona and Madrid. He deplored, among other things, the way politics has been taken hostage by

---

1. Various authors have used the concept of kidnapping to condemn problematic elements affecting democracy. Two examples are Manuel Ayllon's 1997 book and Francisco Rubiales's 2007 book, both titled *Kidnapped Democracy*. Two books titled *The Kidnapping of Democracy* were published by Antonio Piqueras et al. (2011) and by Justino Sinova and Javier Tusell (1990). All of them raise some valuable points; however, none explores the metaphor (components and dynamics) that I attempt to elucidate throughout this volume.

power elites and how a democracy that is unable to resist 'the pressures of economic power to protect its citizens' interests is a feeble democracy' (Mora 2004). Saramago concluded by saying that we are currently living in an obstructed, amputated and hijacked democracy.

The concern Saramago voiced in 2004 seems to have spread to other areas in recent years. Since the emergence of Spain's 15-M movement in 2011, there have been numerous charges that democracy is being held captive by very specific forces. Some platforms closely linked to this movement have actually used the term *kidnapping* in their protests. This was the case of the Platform for People Affected by Mortgages (*Plataforma de Afectados por la Hipoteca – PAH*), which in its struggle to change the Spanish mortgage law, sent a letter to then prime minister Mariano Rajoy affirming that 'when a government elected by the people depends on and pays homage to a financial power that is not comprised of people, it can never be a government of the people or govern on behalf of the people. Democracy has been hijacked and only an organised citizenry can rescue it' (PAH 2013). In Spanish society, it is common to hear voices warning of the concentration of power in the hands of actors who take the entire political system hostage. The 15-M movement – and many other contemporary prodemocracy movements such as Iceland's 'Pots and Pans' revolution, the Arab Spring, the Occupy movement, #YoSoy132 or the Hong Kong protests – all highlight (in addition to their own particular and heterogeneous demands) the need to recover and extend the political capability and influence of citizens (Flesher Fominaya 2014; Della Porta 2013).

The process of progressive and excessive concentration of power in certain hands is also being recognized by journalists. A cursory internet search turns up headlines such as 'No! – to a Hijacked Democracy', 'Hijacked Democracy and Inequality' and 'The Quiet

Coup',[2] revealing a visible rise in the number of articles and opinion pieces with headlines condemning captive democracies.

CONCERN SPREADS TO SOME POLITICIANS AND ECONOMISTS

Voices denouncing the kidnapping of democracy by certain powers are not only increasingly heard among writers, activists and journalists but also among political representatives who are starting to condemn this reality. José Mujica, former guerrilla and later president of Uruguay (2010–2015), said in statements to the media, 'We live in a hijacked democracy that is much worse than a manifest dictatorship' (*La Sexta Noche* 2017). Yanis Varoufakis, former Greek finance minister and university professor, shares similar ideas and is especially critical of how European institutions currently operate. Varoufakis accuses these institutions of initiating a process to depoliticize decision making with the clear objective to relentlessly 'drive towards taking the "demos" out of 'democracy' (Varoufakis 2016).

It is not only openly left-leaning political representatives who have reached such conclusions. Former US president Barack Obama, in his last State of the Union address in 2016, subtly but clearly alluded to some of the problems arising from a gradual concentration of power. Specifically, he stated that 'democracy breaks down when the average person feels their voice doesn't matter; that the system is rigged in favor of the rich or the powerful or some special interest'.[3]

Paradoxically, the shocking and unexpected 2016 election of multimillionaire Donald Trump occurred in circumstances that

---

2. An interesting collection of studies (in Spanish) on elite behaviour and public policies in Latin America is published by the Latin American Council of Social Sciences (CLACSO), http://www.clacso.org.ar/difusion/Resultados_CLACSO_OXFAM/resultados.htm.

3. The transcript of Barack Obama's State of the Union address is available at https://www.nytimes.com/2016/01/13/us/politics/obama-2016-sotu-transcript.html.

have certain parallels (at least in his inaugural speech) with the idea that politics today has been taken hostage by other powers. Trump ran for election on an antiestablishment platform fuelled by constant criticism of the elites, especially the Washington elites. In his inaugural address, Trump went so far as to state that 'today's ceremony, however, has very special meaning. Because today we are not merely transferring power from one Administration to another, or from one party to another – but we are transferring power from Washington, DC, and giving it back to you, the American People'. Later, he concluded, 'What truly matters is not which party controls our government, but whether our government is controlled by the people. January 20th, 2017, will be remembered as the day the people became the rulers of this nation again'.[4]

Trump's speech is full of criticism of the system and the loss of the people's (and their representatives') capacity for political action. Trump in the United States, Wilders in Holland and Le Pen in France are among those who have incorporated in their analyses (and in their aggressive speeches) the notion of a deficient democracy due to the colonization of the political sphere by powerful sectors, and by other organizations such as insurers, the European Union and the International Monetary Fund. This part of their analyses (and only this part) concurs with the other actors discussed in this section, although it is clear that their ideals, solutions and proposals are radically different from the other opinions included here.

Importantly, not only political representatives but also economists are among the numerous voices warning of a captive democracy. I will refer to various specialists in this field throughout this book; however, it is interesting to note in this first chapter the opinion of Simon Johnson, a former chief economist for the International Monetary Fund (IMF). In 2009, Johnson wrote a contro-

---

4. Remarks of President Donald J. Trump (20 January 2017), *The Inaugural Address*. Retrieved from https://www.whitehouse.gov/briefings-statements/the-inaugural-address/ (accessed 21 March 2019).

versial magazine article, 'The Quiet Coup', a title that provides many clues as to the nature of his critique. In this piece, Johnson sounds the alarm about an elite of financiers (especially in the United States) 'against which the government seems helpless, or unwilling, to act' (2009). The former IMF chief says of the United States, 'Just as we have the world's most advanced economy, military, and technology, we also have its most advanced oligarchy' (Johnson 2009). Johnson expresses concern about a series of threats facing democracy today and condemns, from the very heart of such a powerful organization as the IMF, the formation of oligarchies capable of systematically imposing specific policies designed to benefit themselves.

Thus, the perception of the progressive and excessive concentration of power by certain groups (which hinders, limits and obscures any hope of a true separation of powers) has begun to spread, although no one has yet claimed responsibility for the kidnapping. Having heard some of the voices sounding the alarm, we must now identify the hostages.

2

THE HOSTAGES (I)

Political Parties and Governments

When a kidnapping occurs and is made public, attention immediately turns to the hostages, who have lost their freedom and all capacity to act. The victims are at the mercy of their captors' whims, considered merely as 'merchandise' to exchange for money, or in the case of politically motivated kidnappings, pawns to force certain decisions. Unfortunately, both forms of kidnapping are very familiar to us today.

Examples of kidnappings for financial gain abound. An especially notorious case in Spain was the kidnapping of Maria Angels Feliu, a pharmacist who was confined to a very small underground pit for fourteen months until her release in March 1994.[1] The pursuit of financial reward is the main motive for this type of kidnapping. In some countries this practice has become so common that it is impossible to estimate exactly how many cases occur each year as only a small percentage is reported. In some places

---

1. The kidnappers demanded a ransom for Feliu; however, she was eventually freed by one of her kidnappers and no money was handed over.

'express' kidnappings for ransom are so widespread that they are conducted as a line of 'business'.[2]

Politically motivated kidnappings are less common but there have been many incidences of terrorist groups kidnapping someone (often a political figure) to force a situation or decision. Some cases, such as the 1975 abduction of Peter Lorenz in West Berlin by the 2 June movement, end with an agreement and the release of the hostage (Lorenz was freed in exchange for the release of Red Army Faction prisoners). On other occasions, however, the kidnapping ends in tragedy, such as the cases of Aldo Moro in Italy in 1978 and Miguel Angel Blanco in Spain in 1997, both of whom were murdered by their kidnappers, the Red Brigades and the Basque separatist group ETA, respectively.

In addition to financially and politically motivated kidnappings, sexual exploitation and abuse can be the incentive for other forms of forcible capture. Notorious cases include that of Elisabeth Fritzl, who from 1984 to 2008 suffered at the hands of her own father, labelled in the international media as the Monster of Amstetten (Austria). During her captivity, the victim gave birth to seven children as a result of sexual abuse and rape. Other examples of this type of kidnapping include the cases of Natascha Maria Kampusch, held captive in Austria from 1998 to 2006, or Lydia Gouardo, confined from 1975 to 1999 in France.

Each type of kidnapping (indeed, each individual kidnapping) has its own specific characteristics and embodies situations of great drama, as evidenced in the many heartrending personal accounts of those who have been deprived of their freedom by the

---

2. The study by Llorens and Moreno on kidnappings in Latin America finds that the approximately 7,500 cases reported each year represent only one-tenth of the actual kidnappings (Llorens and Moreno 2008, 12). The authors note that this crime has reached shocking levels in countries such as Mexico, Colombia, Brazil and Argentina, and that it is also on the rise in Haiti, Venezuela, Ecuador, Peru and Paraguay. Other sources such as *Mexico Denuncia* claim there were over 32,000 kidnappings in Mexico alone during 2015. See http://www.mexicodenuncia.or/?page_id=103 (in Spanish).

coercive force of their kidnappers.[3] The hostage frequently becomes a mere instrument to be 'used' by kidnappers who arbitrarily decide their fate and fortune.

When these reflections are applied to the field of democracy, some basic differences emerge. The victim is not a person. In this case, institutions are held hostage by a series of captors. These institutions – naturally comprised of people – also lose all ability to manoeuvre and freedom to act. When the basic structures of the democratic system are hijacked, we reach a point where the form and appearance of democracy are maintained, but it is devoid of content. This condition stifles any possibility of applying a wide range of diverse options and enables the kidnappers to surreptitiously impose a uniform type of policy. In addition, as mentioned in the previous chapter, the hijacking of democracy is not accompanied by the public outcry over kidnappings with political or financial motives intended to grip the public's attention.

As if that were not enough, the kidnapping of democracy also shares another significant facet with sexual exploitation kidnappings. The reward the kidnappers are seeking is not a ransom but control over their hostages for as long a period as possible. In this case, no ransom is demanded in exchange for the hostages' release, since the kidnappers' objective is to prolong and conceal the situation. As with other kidnappings, the hostages are in considerable danger and are being used instrumentally; however, their situation is much less conspicuous than that of someone with a ransom on their head. This leads to the vital question of exactly which institutions are being held hostage in this process.

In attempting to answer this question we could begin by considering the kidnapping of democracy as a complex phenomenon, involving various victims and diverse mechanisms to hold them

---

3. Llorens and Moreno's (2008) book, *El secuestro en Latinoaméric: Los ojos de la víctima* [*Kidnapping in Latin America: In the eyes of the victim*], is a rich source of information on the tragedy of dozens of kidnapping victims. Other books that graphically illustrate the drama of kidnappings are *News of a Kidnapping* by Gabriel García Márquez (1997) and Ingrid Betancourt's (2010) autobiographical *Even Silence Has an End: My Six Years of Captivity in the Colombian Jungle*.

captive. However, perhaps a better way to start unravelling this phenomenon is to first identify the main (or some of the main) institutions of a democratic system and clarify what we expect from them as citizens. In other words, by reflecting on these institutions when they are 'free', we may be in a position to assess their current state of abduction.

THE MINIMUM REQUIREMENTS FOR A FREE (REPRESENTATIVE) DEMOCRACY

Today, democracy enjoys undisputed legitimacy as the best available political system (or, for the more pessimistic, the 'least bad'). However, there are many different ways of interpreting and implementing this ideal, based on the 'power of the *demos*'. This has attracted debate in political theory and philosophy for centuries, much of which concerns just how much power or decision-making ability should be redistributed across the political community and how this redistribution should occur (Sartori 2009; García Marzá 1993). In this line, proposals from democratic theory on the amount of political responsibility to allocate to the *demos* cover a wide spectrum of options ranging from the least demanding and most elitist to the most demanding and most participatory (with a wide variety of options in between). This book is not the context in which to fully explore this very broad debate; however, our analysis does require some reflection on the minimum requirements demanded by current models of representative democracy. At this point, we only present what are known as models of minimal democracy and leave the more participatory forms of democracy for further discussion (chapter 9).

One of the seminal works on this model of democracy is *Capitalism, Socialism and Democracy*, published in 1942 by the economist and thinker Joseph Schumpeter. This author was sceptical of citizens' ability to participate in political affairs, to the point of claiming that 'the typical citizen drops down to a lower level of mental performance as soon as he enters the political field'

(Schumpeter 2003, 261). His particular assessment of the public's 'potential' in public affairs led him to propose a model of democracy based on competitive selection among representatives. Schumpeter's proposal is defined as a 'democratic method' understood as an 'institutional arrangement for arriving at political decisions in which individuals acquire the power to decide by means of a competitive struggle for the people's vote' (2003, 242). Therefore, democracy only means that the people have the opportunity to accept or reject those who aspire to govern them.

Despite this reductionist view of democracy based on the idea that 'democracy is the rule of the politician' (2003, 285), Schumpeter also established what he believed to be a wholly realistic set of minimum conditions. These requirements include the need to develop highly trained (both intellectually and morally) representatives, to have multiple political options and to foster both an effective rotation of leaders and representatives with a decisive ability to act (Schumpeter 2003).

Robert Dahl, another renowned writer on democracy theory, also viewed democracy as a method for selecting leaders and governments, although he expanded Schumpeter's basic requirements to include the development of what he called polyarchy, a government 'of the many' (Dahl 2008). In this system, elections would guarantee balance of power and accountability, as well as freedom of speech, autonomous associations and an inclusive citizenry (Dahl 1989).

These alternative forms of democracy, both minimalist and elitist models of democracy, focus on representation in the political process and start from the basic premise that citizens must have the right to choose their representatives (organized in political parties), who must be free to make decisions affecting the region they govern. Leaders are expected to reach binding decisions through dialogue and negotiation with other political parties, and at the same time represent many diverse interests. Political parties must be capable of reflecting society's multiple perspectives and perceptions and transferring them to its institutions. They must carry out their duties competently and remain separate from other centres of power. This democratic system grants citizens limited power, although they are at least able to reward or punish their representatives at the polls by choosing from a wide range of political representatives. This model of democracy, as conceived by authors such as Schumpeter and Dahl (and many other thinkers), is the basis for the political system implemented and developed in the West. Freedom of action for political parties and governments is an essential condition for this system. In other words, for the system to operate smoothly, representatives must be able to make independent decisions without interference, and they must have the freedom to follow diverse political programmes; this is the only way to guarantee that certain interests in society are not forced upon others, or at least restrain their overt dominance. By saying this, I am not denying the complexity of the political environment, riddled as it is with strain, problems and tensions. Indeed, to quote Foucault who, in turn, inverted Clausewitz's phrase, politics has often been described as 'the continuation of war by other means'.[4] We cannot expect the state to be completely free from the institutions of a representative democracy (if that were even possible); however, the situation that I am describing here is precisely the opposite: almost complete captivity.

At the same time, other institutions play a vital role in representative democracy. The media, for example, shapes public opinion and is necessary to counterbalance the economic and political sphere; trade unions represent workers' interests in negotiations with the business sector, and social movements and nongovernmental organizations (NGOs) provide spaces for civic society to self-organize and apply pressure. Without these institutions, the balance of power and interests – or Dahl's polyarchy – can be threatened by a 'government of a (very) few'. Each institution – political parties, governments, the media, trade unions – carries out its own function and citizens have different expectations of them, but we expect all of them to have some degree of autonomy

---

4. The nineteenth-century Prussian military theorist Carl von Clausewitz defined war as 'the continuation of politics by other means'.

and to guarantee the representation of multiple interests. In short, we assume they will not be taken over by another power.

DEMOCRACY TODAY

It is not easy to diagnose the health of these institutions or to assess their public approval or disapproval. However, a wide range of tools and resources can give us some indications of their strengths or weaknesses. Political science and sociology can help us in this assessment, while sources such as the Eurobarometer or the Organisation for Economic Co-operation and Development (OECD) reports[5] assess the degree of trust citizens have in the political parties, governments, mass media and civic society in their countries.

This amount of information cannot easily be summarized in a few sentences. However, some authors have analysed the data, revealing a clear upward trend of widespread disaffection, especially with representative structures. This trend – with contextual nuances and idiosyncrasies – can be observed across Western liberal democratic systems. An illuminating explanation for this pattern is provided by Peter Mair in his book *Ruling the Void: The Hollowing of Western Democracy*, a comparative study of electoral participation in recent decades. Mair's study demonstrates a general increase in citizens' disaffection towards representative structures and elections. He also shows that those who do still turn out to vote are more unpredictable in their voting patterns due to the increasingly weak commitment to one political party, thus making election result predictions an ever more difficult task. He also identifies a significant decline in party affiliation in recent decades, indicating that parties are losing much of the public loyalty they enjoyed in the past.

What Mair finds most striking is that, despite its nuances and differences, this trend is repeated in every ostensibly stable West-

---

5.   See http://www.oecd.org/gov/trust-in-government.htm.

ern democracy. He also expresses concern about the growing distance between the public and the political class due to a process of mutual withdrawal in which 'citizens retreat into private life or into more specialised and often ad hoc forms of representation, and whereby the party leaderships retreat into the institutions, drawing their terms of reference ever more readily from their roles as governors or public-office holders' (Mair 2005, 8; see also Mair 2013). This is precisely the dynamic that causes the progressive banalization and hollowing of Western democracy.

The British author Colin Crouch, who coined the term *postdemocracy*, also contemplates these worrisome trends in a decaying political system. His work mostly explores the dark side of globalization and the mounting difficulties of imposing checks and balances on transnational elites. He also condemns the inability of political parties to understand what the public wants, which ultimately reduces parties to mere tools for capturing votes that do not effectively represent the interests of the people. For Crouch, democracy today has thus become nothing more than a 'spectacle that is tightly controlled and managed by rival teams of professionals who are experts in the techniques of persuasion, and that focuses only on a small range of issues chosen by these teams' (Crouch 2004, 4). He goes on to state that in this postdemocratic landscape, major political decisions are made 'behind the scenes by elected governments interacting with elites that overwhelmingly represent business interests' (Crouch 2004, 4). In sum, Crouch concludes that the 'interests of a minority' count more than 'a group of ordinary people' (2004, 19) who are abandoned with no representation.

Crouch's thesis helps us understand some basic aspects of today's democratic system, such as the lack of representation of diverse interests or the rise of de facto powers whose influence goes far beyond the economic realm. A few years before Crouch's book, Carl Boggs reproached the colonization of politics by large corporations in another provocative and enlightening volume, *The End of Politics* (Boggs 2001). In this study of the United States, Boggs warned how certain decadent trends were eroding the public sphere, trends that today seem to be well-established in many Western representative democracies. His analysis and primary concern focuses on the growing depoliticization of the public due to the absence of viable alternatives and the hidden power of certain elites.

These studies provide a necessary framework to continue our discussion on kidnapped democracy, together with a deeper critique that attempts to identify the kidnappers and the hostages (the puzzle I hope to unravel throughout the chapters of this book). It is also useful to consider the varied responses of the kidnapping 'victims', which seem to go beyond the passive attitude of the public described by Crouch and Boggs (in later chapters I outline several responses, ranging from Stockholm syndrome to attempted rebellion). However, at this point in the story, it is important to note that authors such as Mair, Boggs and Crouch help us recognize something that as citizens we already sense: that even the minimum requirements of the least demanding models of democracy are currently far from being satisfied. In other words, serious cracks can be seen in the central foundations of representative democracy. One of the most problematic aspects is the lack of freedom facing such crucial institutions as governments and political parties. These institutions are the focus of the following section.

POLITICAL PARTIES AND GOVERNMENTS AS HOSTAGES

If there is one institution that comes out badly in Metroscope's opinion polls – and not just in one country – it is the political party. The party political structure plays a fundamental and determining role in our democracies, but it is experiencing very significant levels of disaffection and indifference. This is not a new phenomenon, however; as far back as the early twentieth century scholars were already wondering how this institution had lost its way. This was one theme in Robert Michels's book, first published in 1911,

Political Parties: A Sociological Study of the Oligarchical Tenden-
cies of Modern Democracy. Michels warned that we should not be
overoptimistic about political organizations and their future and
believed that they could not escape what he called 'the iron law of
oligarchy' (2001, 224). This law prevents political parties from
functioning according to democratic logic since their very nature
propels them to becoming electoral machines or, as Michels says,
a 'methodical organisation of the electoral masses' (Michels 2001,
219). The more a party grows, the more bureaucratized it becomes and the more it focuses on the sole objective of attaining
political power. In this process a schism develops inside the party,
dividing the constituency from internal leadership, and eventually
resulting in its gradual estrangement from the entire populace.

Michels's work remains an important reference that can be
applied to address some of the current problems affecting political
parties, especially regarding their internal dynamics. The 'iron law
of oligarchy' theory helps us to understand how easily political
parties can fall under the spell of their own rationale and internal
struggles. However, political parties are now also threatened by
another form of hijacking – this time from external sources. Parties have become hostages not only to themselves, but also to
other forces that have exploited their needs and weaknesses. By
doing so, the kidnappers have subjugated the political parties so
that rather than serving the electorate (or at least part of it), they
are used to serve the kidnappers' own purposes.

Political Parties Adrift

The electoral process is now shifting towards (and reduced to) a
highly competitive dynamic. As described in the previous chapter,
Schumpeter hoped that in this process the parties would present
diverse choices and 'quality' candidates, thus leading to the selection of 'the best', a process in which the diverse interests of society
would be represented. However, the intensity of electoral competition today requires an endless stream of financial reserves to

maintain both party and election machinery, which has turned fundraising into an essential activity. Furthermore, the desire to win elections leads parties to pursue sufficiently large (and also ambiguous) niche voting blocs that allow them to gain power. For some time, political theorists have warned of the impact that the mass media (especially television) can have on electoral processes in which 'serious' political parties, committed to the debate of ideas, and with conscientious electoral programmes, gradually turn into 'brand-oriented' political parties that use emotion to promote their image (Sartori 1989; McAllister 2007; Crouch 2004). Today we continue to see what are often energetic, passionate and heated electoral debates in which political parties compete for votes. However, the differences between the parties on critical questions and general commitments are narrowing (Dalton and Wattenberg 2002; Alonso 2014), and debates are much more concerned with form than content. Thus, the political races we witness increasingly resemble, in the words of Wolfgang Streeck, 'the type of competition that is seen in football matches or horse races: energetic, exciting, and even attractive to spectators, but ultimately lacking any significance of substance' (2011, 82).

Research on political manifestos has revealed a convergence of the right and left since the 1980s, to the extent that it is increasingly difficult for these platforms to 'maintain distinct identities' (Caul and Gray 2002, 235; see also Gray and Caul 2000). Some comparative empirical studies have even concluded that we are going through a period of 'disappearing partisan effects' (Huber and Stephens 2001, 321).

Different elements play different roles in the consolidation of this spreading phenomenon. On one hand, parties' desire and ambition to hold on to or increase their power and power structures are in large part responsible for their current loss of direction. On the other hand, the hijackers of democracy, the focus of chapter 5, are keenly aware of these needs and weaknesses and exploit them to the full for their own benefit. A party needs votes and media influence, and to secure them it relies heavily on money and influence. The kidnappers use these weaknesses to weave a web of dependency that forces parties to rely on them. The financing of political parties, which often depend on liquidity and close relationships between the financial and political sectors (revolving doors are one of the most obvious manifestations of this), has come at a high cost to political autonomy and has resulted in the political sphere opening its doors wide to colonization from certain economic sectors.

Governments in Chains

These are not the only difficulties facing the parties: their problems are exacerbated when the time comes to form or lead governments. Added to their ambitions, temptations and internal power struggles – all easily exploited by kidnappers – political parties must also contend with the recent surge in the globalization process, a task that seems to be completely beyond their grasp. Globalization has dramatically reduced distances of space and time across the planet, and has coincided with the development of a host of unparalleled technological and communication devices. However, this has also led to the rapid ascent of transnational economic powers, compared to the much more tentative, or even nonexistent, emergence of political institutions with the same global reach (González Esteban 2013). In other words, despite the advantages and potential of this process, huge challenges have also arisen from the significant shortcomings in political regulation, which can easily be exploited by economically powerful transnational groups (Rodrik 2011). While the sphere of influence of political parties and governments is generally limited to the national level, these economically powerful groups know no bounds. We are therefore faced with a situation in which political autonomy is seriously threatened by the imperatives and mandates of a globalization process characterized by increasing deregulation of the economic and financial system, which only increases its power to the detriment of political power (Kocka 2016).

In recent years, economists, scientists and political theorists have attempted to explain these trends and their development in past decades. Similarly, there is widespread agreement that the 2008 global crisis marked a turning point that some have called the definitive 'coup'. In this vein, Streeck notes that since the start of the crisis, distributional conflict has further complicated the 'tug-of-war between global financial investors and sovereign nation-states' (2011, 21). Other authors such as Pierre Dardot and Christian Laval define this moment as a 'change in direction' that used more sophisticated strategies to defend the interests of the elites (2019). In their book *Never Ending Nightmare*, these authors discuss how after 2008, the oligarchy has managed to establish 'crisis government', a strategy the economic and financial elites use to impose their own remedies, crushing all resistance from political actors. They do this by weaponizing external financing, such that when governments need to access finance, they must first accept the conditions the oligarchy imposes. Streeck explains this pressure as follows: 'Today no government can ignore international constraints and obligations, including those from financial markets that force nations to impose sacrifices on their people' (2011, 24). In circumstances where it is difficult to operate exclusively in the domestic sphere, the tense relationship between the economy and politics tips the balance towards the former.

Therefore, as cautioned in chapter 1, it is no surprise to hear extensive condemnation of the pressure the markets impose on democracy – markets that are intransigent in dictating the policies that the governments of nation-states must approve or reject. It is now paradoxical that the Manhattan-based rating agencies which were instrumental in causing the 2008 financial disaster now threaten to downgrade the ratings of state debt securities as a device for imposing very specific economic prescriptions.

Thus, not only do political parties lose freedom and room to manoeuvre, but governments are also victims of their internal 'weaknesses' as political parties (their determination to hold on to power through perpetual reelection, their new status as products of advertising, etc.) and of external factors against which they are defenceless or impotent, especially given the transnational nature of economic powers. This trend can easily be seen in the countries of southern Europe, for example. Spain's socialist government amended its constitution in August 2011 almost overnight, with the support of the People's Party (Partido Popular), a highly unusual move by political parties that aggressively resist any constitutional change under most circumstances. The revised constitution established a budget stability measure in which public debt repayment was prioritized over any other type of budget expenditure. This measure was expressly designed to satisfy the financial markets. However, even strong economies such as Germany face the same pressures, turning them into 'hostages' of other actors. The economist Streeck relates how Chancellor Merkel's attempt in early 2010 to redistribute certain costs resulting from the economic crisis provoked suggestions that 'perhaps the creditors should also pay part of the cost'. These voices were soon silenced as soon as 'the markets' reacted by slightly raising the interest rate on German public debt (2011, 25).

Although, as we will see later, there are exceptions to such political capitulation, numerous examples abound of governments facing enormous obstacles to the free implementation of policies, not only in Europe but also in other Western democracies. Their need to obtain financing in globalized, international markets makes them easy prey. Some academics even think governments have lost not only the ability to manage the economy but also their intent and desire to do so (Scharpf 2000). This would explain the waves of deregulation and privatization that have merely served to reinforce the kidnapping of democracy in recent decades.

This trend translates into a clear loss of flexibility for basic representative structures such as political parties and governments. It reinforces an overt prejudice towards citizens, who suffer the worst consequences of institutional hijacking in the form of cutbacks in public services, the cost of bank bailouts, state bankruptcies and higher interest rates on public debt.

Furthermore, it is easy to understand how these dynamics lead people to perceive that they are no longer represented by their governments. Thus, governments and political parties are gradually stripped of their representative identity (Tormey 2015). Citizens no longer feel represented because they can see whose interests are really defended in this unequal, imbalanced relationship. The electorate is also acutely aware of the paucity of real electoral choices on offer when the occasion comes around every four or five years. The decisions that are finally taken in their parliaments are predetermined or imposed by external entities that are not answerable to the public and over which the people have no control whatsoever. The public has little chance of asserting its inter ests through the parties because today, economic power is also political power.

Having seen how political parties and governments have come adrift, I now ask where other basic pillars of democratic systems like the media and journalists stand in this regard. Can we expect them to take responsibility for condemning these kidnappings or, on the contrary, are they also facing challenges and problems that shackle their democratizing potential?

.

3

THE HOSTAGES (II)

The Mass Media

In a kidnapping, the hostage takers establish strategic contacts with various actors, including not only the hostages, family members and security forces, but also the media. In these cases, journalism plays a vital yet complex role. It is the journalist's basic duty to report the facts and context of a situation, but this task is not without its challenges. They must respect the dignity of the hostages, guard against being used as a mouthpiece by the kidnappers or representing their interests, and avoid jeopardizing the work of the investigators and law enforcement officers on the kidnappers' trail.

In politically motivated kidnappings, the media's role is crucial since they could potentially be manipulated to put pressure on public opinion, governments and negotiators, or be used as a channel to communicate the kidnappers' positions or demands. In financially motivated kidnappings, the hostage takers might also exploit media channels to intensify relatives' anxiety and force a ransom negotiation. Kidnappers deliberately plan their relationships with the media in advance, and in consequence journalists must be acutely aware of their responsibilities and their powerful position in the situation. They can play a key role in framing and condemning the event, or they can end up helping the kidnappers, albeit involuntarily.

The hijackers of democracy are clearly aware of the power of the media and the fundamental role they play in the political system. The media have the capacity to help liberate democracy by uncovering the kidnappers' identities, strategies and their hidden interests. It is therefore now appropriate to ask ourselves what role we a priori associate with the media in an established democracy and then assess whether they actually fulfil this function.

A FREE MASS MEDIA

The crucial role of the media and journalism in an established democracy has been extensively studied by scholars in the fields of communications, sociology, philosophy and political science, and it is widely acknowledged by the public. Journalism and the media provide the basis on which citizens can compare and substantiate the information they need to reach informed opinions, thereby validating what is commonly known as public opinion. Even minimalist or elitist models of democracy, limited to the basic electoral process, defend the key role of the media since they expect citizens to exercise their power at the polls responsibly. For this reason, authors such as Sartori state that the machine operators who pull the levers in the democratic machinery – the electorate – must be able to develop their own informed opinions on the electoral process (Sartori 2009). From a deliberative view of democracy, Habermas also defends the importance of a highly informed body of public opinion that can reason and discuss matters of public interest and influence public decision-making entities. These aspects therefore imply that journalism and the media are 'the backbone' of a democracy and act as intermediaries between society and its political agents (Habermas 1996).

In addition to nurturing a highly informed body of public opinion, the media has another vital task: holding the centres of power accountable. We expect journalists to rigorously monitor the spaces where decisions are made and sound the alarm when they detect any lack of transparency, abuse of power, or malpractice. For this reason, the media are often understood as a counterweight to power, a space for auditing and monitoring economic and political spheres where decisions affecting thousands or even millions of people are made. The obvious essential precondition for this task is media and journalistic independence. Only when their autonomy from the centres of power is guaranteed can they fulfil their function and role as guardians in their reporting. Precisely for this reason, respected journalists Bill Kovach and Tom Rosenstiel, in their book *The Elements of Journalism*, reiterate the importance of journalistic independence and separation from centres of power (2007). A free press allows citizens to obtain sufficient information to shape well-informed public opinion and ensures any hijacking of democracy is roundly condemned. But is this actually happening?

JOURNALISM AND THE MEDIA: POWERFUL BUT HEAVILY CONSTRAINED

As we will see later (especially in chapter 9), it would be unfair and mistaken to claim that independent or investigative journalism has disappeared in recent decades. That said, certain problems are severely affecting editorial independence. Journalism is currently facing numerous challenges and difficulties, including the rise of large global media conglomerates, the transition to digital, falling advertising revenue, the surfeit of information, and increased job insecurity. Perhaps one of the most worrying problems is the gradual concentration of media ownership in the hands of a few large conglomerates as a result of the mergers and acquisitions of large companies. This process directly threatens any democratic system that purports to guarantee a diverse range of voices and media in the public sphere.

Robert McChesney, a leading theorist in the field of communication, uses the concept of 'rich media, poor democracy' to highlight this worrying situation (2015). McChesney warns that the media giants have never been bigger, and their influence has grown proportionally. Control and command of the media cannot be separated from the debate on the current state of democracy.

The large media conglomerates began to develop after World War II, but this trend intensified in the late 1980s. Changes in laws and new regulations have since strengthened the media giants we know today (Herman and McChesney 1997). It may seem a preposterous notion that one person could hold control over dozens of newspapers and magazines in the United States, United Kingdom and Australia with one company and over several television networks with another. This is no fantasy, however; communications tycoon Rupert Murdoch now controls a massive media conglomerate in multiple national markets, a position that places him in a position of dominant influence (Flew 2007). The media and political power of today's media giants such as News Corporation, Comcast and Bertelsmann is significant.

Similarly, media ownership has become highly complex; in parallel to the corporate consolidation of media ownership, a specific profile of the media company shareholder has also emerged. One example affecting the Spanish-speaking world (and especially Spain) is that of the PRISA Group, whose shareholders include banks such as HSBC, Santander and CaixaBank; large companies like Telefónica; powerful business magnates; and several vulture hedge funds. The same can be said of the other big media groups.

The consolidation of communications giants, together with powerful shareholders from the business world, has brought us to the point where a handful of people effectively 'own' the information and can decide which topics merit media analysis. At the same time, the wide range of media companies is, nonetheless, very homogeneous. Despite the apparent abundance of communications channels, essential news is frequently ignored or voices silenced when information is uncovered that media owners want to keep hidden. The small number of mass media moguls cramps rigorous, independent journalism, and democracy suffers as a result.

The mass media and journalists almost inevitably reflect the interests of their paymasters and thereby act as spokespersons for the hijackers of democracy and their interests. In short, far from offering hope to democracy today, the kidnappers hold the media as high-value hostages, just as they do the political parties and governments.

4

THE HOSTAGES (III)

Trade Unions

The threat of a kidnapped democracy also extends to another pillar of democracy: trade unions. These organizations play a fundamental role as intermediaries between diverse interests and in pursuing the balance of power. Because active and effective trade unions are a potential threat to any actor wanting to seize and colonize the political sphere, it is necessary to examine the current state of affairs in these institutions.

THE ROLE OF TRADE UNIONS

Trade unions are a key component of our political systems, acting on behalf of workers' interests by ensuring professional, workplace and social rights through negotiation with employers and governments. Their chief concern is the welfare of workers, which they aim to guarantee by defending and fighting for decent working conditions. As a society, we expect unions to act as representatives that can deliver fair contracts and collective agreements through dialogue and negotiation with businesses and governments. Naturally, such negotiations can be tense and may lead to the use of tactics to put pressure on the other party, such as a strike action or breaking off negotiations. However, both sides are expected to represent the interests of their respective constituents to best effect. The social legitimacy of the trade union depends precisely on whether its affiliates believe it is really defending their interests and whether this defence is effective. However, in these times of austerity and globalization is this actually happening? Are the unions acting freely and effectively, or are there signs that the stealthy hijacking of democracy is also affecting these institutions?

THE UNMET CHALLENGE OF GLOBALIZATION

Despite their importance, trade unions are living through tumultuous times in many parts of the world, and they now seem to be a long way from their heyday when they successfully negotiated collective agreements and enjoyed widespread social legitimacy. Like the political parties, unions are facing new challenges. In the wake of the Great Recession of 2008, social contracts have come under threat, and unions are no longer the guests of honour at the negotiating table, even in the countries most affected by the crisis. These countries have been compelled to introduce measures of 'economic rationalization', in the euphemistic style of Orwell's 'newspeak', or cutbacks, to use a less cynical, more direct term.

In recent years the governments of countries such as Spain and Italy have come under pressure from international organizations like the European Central Bank to implement measures such as public spending cuts. In other countries, Portugal and Greece for example, the troika's[1] even harsher interventions have included swingeing spending cuts, drastic reductions in the number of people covered by collective agreements and reductions to the minimum wage. Trade unions in these countries have proved incapable of challenging these policies. Measures imposed by govern-

---

1. The troika refers to the European Commission (EC), the European Central Bank (ECB) and the International Monetary Fund (IMF).

ments and international organizations through the rescue programmes for the Eurozone countries have complicated the unions' work enormously, as well as greatly reducing their scope of activity and political influence.

This phenomenon is also linked to globalization, which inevitably has an impact on the entire trade union movement. Trade unions are rooted in nation-states, which as noted above, have been weakened by globalization. Governments and states have lost much of their power to negotiate and offer concessions in the new dynamic of global competition (Upchurch, Taylor and Mathers 2009). The loss of freedom suffered by governments and political parties (chapter 2) directly affects the way trade unions operate because they depend on these entities being able to enter into negotiations.

In addition, the unions have recently come under attack and faced ridicule in an aggressive narrative spun by the mass media. This narrative should come as no surprise, given the ownership of the large media conglomerates and where their interests lie (chapter 3).

The curbing of the unions' ability to act in conjunction with these attacks has undermined the legitimacy of this key actor in the political system and throws some light on some of the reasons for the overall decline in union membership (in the United Kingdom, union membership has almost halved since the 1980s) and for the erosion of their perceived social legitimacy. However, these are external factors; internal factors for which unions are directly responsible have also played their part.

INTERNAL WEAKNESSES

Not all unions find themselves in the same situation, however, and their levels of membership and social legitimacy vary widely, although scholars have noted a generalized decline in union membership and their perceived legitimacy in recent years (Upchurch, Taylor and Mathers 2009; Bernaciak, Gumbrell-McCormick and

Hyman 2014). As an institution, trade unions face many tough challenges. As well as globalization, they have felt the impact of other transformations such as deindustrialization, technological – especially digital – developments, diversification of employment models, new forms of labour organization and a certain weakening of the identity of the worker. None of these challenges is easily tackled.

In addition, any serious analysis must also acknowledge that, as well as these external challenges and factors, the unions have failed to address other problems as a result of their internal dynamics and inaction. For example, in response to the Eurozone crisis, a clearly transnational question, the unions remained firmly entrenched in their own nation-state arenas. Furthermore, during citizen protests against austerity measures, leadership from the unions was conspicuous by their absence. Although they eventually joined in and supported these movements, they did not take up a leadership position to represent workers' interests as they had in the past. Indeed, many citizen movements have harshly criticized the unions for their lack of engagement, their close ties with government, their narrow-mindedness, their lethargy and their lack of transparency.

An interesting study on the current state of the unions by Pepper Culpepper and Aidan Regan (2014) offers a detailed analysis of the cases of Italy and Ireland in an attempt to understand the conditions necessary for unions to succeed in their negotiation processes. Their study compares trade union performance in recent decades and concludes that in the 1990s unions were highly successful in mobilizing their members and reaching agreements with and obtaining concessions from government and business. The authors note that the main reason for these accomplishments is that both public opinion and the elites regarded the unions as 'representatives of all those who depend on a job to make a living' (Culpepper and Regan 2014, 728). They were not viewed as a specific interest group but as representatives of all workers. Both government and employers acknowledged the unions' legitimacy and they were highly respected for their ability to mobilize. In cases of dispute, employers feared financial losses and political parties feared electoral repercussions. The unions also contributed to political, social and economic stability by explaining to their members the sometimes tortuous agreements negotiated with governments and employers. In short, the political and business communities had a clear incentive to reach agreements with the unions.

Culpepper and Regan argue that this successful arrangement disappeared after the 1990s not only because of immediate circumstantial factors but also because of the unions' own internal weaknesses: the unions have been unable to adapt their strategies and dynamics to the current 'post-national' and 'post-industrial' context. Today, they adopt defensive positions, a strategy that means they are perceived as merely another interest group with a heavy focus on its own survival as an organization. They no longer come across as the foremost legitimate representatives of the working class. The decline in membership and legitimacy in turn limits their capacity for action and influence. For this reason, political parties and businesses no longer welcome them to the negotiating table when new policies and measures are discussed, thereby triggering a vicious circle.

In addition to the external factors (globalization, economic crisis, new employment models), the unions seem to have ignored a number of other factors. Their failure to come up with alternative models or adjust to a globalized environment, the lack of new and inclusive forms of membership, and their concession to – and even complicity with – the stringent measures imposed on the population are some of the reasons for the public's loss of faith in yet another key institution of the political system. The unions have unquestionably been taken hostage in the present hijacking of democracy, just like the political parties, governments and the media. The power of the kidnappers has overwhelmed them, suffocating their ability to act, thus provoking their crisis of legitimacy. However, the unions themselves have clearly contributed to this (or at least they have failed to prevent it), which raises questions about their role in the hijacking of politics, questions that can be put to all of the hostages in this captive democracy: political parties, governments and media. We must now ask whether they are just hostages, or accomplices in their own fate, whether they have to some extent willingly sown the seeds of this unfortunate destiny.

5

HOSTAGES OR ACCOMPLICES?

In the various types of kidnappings mentioned earlier (for political motives, financial extortion or sexual abuse), the main victim is the hostage who directly suffers the effects of the crime, although the consequences of a kidnapping are felt by all of the victim's family, friends and immediate circle. They must bear the anxiety about the well-being of their loved one and, like the hostage, the impotence of being at the mercy of the kidnapper's phone calls, demands and final decision. In her book *El secuestro de los Born* (*The Born Kidnapping*), journalist Maria O'Donnell records the testimony of businessman Jorge Born,[1] held captive for more than nine months by the Argentine Montoneros guerrilla group. Several passages reflect on the suffering of people close to the victims, as in this one:

> When he was reunited with his loved ones, Jorge Born had a strange feeling: he had been the kidnapping victim, he had spent nine months locked in a tiny hovel, but he saw the impact of his odyssey much more in others than in himself. Especially in his father. (O'Donnell 2016, 221)

---

1. Businessmen Jorge and Juan Born were kidnapped in 1975 in a case known as 'the most expensive kidnapping in history', which ended with their release in exchange for 60 million US dollars, among other forms of payment.

The consequences and repercussions of a crime as complex as a kidnapping have far-reaching effects on a range of people. The hostages and those close to them live through an intense situation in which the outcome is uncertain and potentially dramatic. In kidnappings for political motives, financial extortion and sexual exploitation, the hostages are in no measure responsible for their predicament. They have no say in their fate, which is decided by others. A hostage can never be held responsible for his or her own captivity. The highly publicized six-year kidnapping of Ingrid Betancourt by the FARC began in 2002 when she was travelling to a demilitarized zone as a presidential candidate to establish peace talks with the FARC guerrillas, circumstances that raised questions from some about her own responsibility for the kidnapping.[2] Whatever the circumstances, however, in such crimes only the kidnappers are in a position to make decisions and must therefore take responsibility for those decisions. Betancourt was a victim like any other and was in no way responsible for her own bad 'luck'. But as the hijacking of democracy affects and involves an infinite number of groups and individuals, several questions remain: Do political parties, governments, the media and trade unions bear any responsibility for this situation? If so, then who are the real victims?

THE TRUE VICTIMS OF KIDNAPPING

A kidnapping can include many different scenarios, and some may even be considered self-kidnappings or hoax kidnappings. Take a situation, for example, in which parents report the kidnapping of

---

2.   One of the accusations was that Betancourt's imprudence led to her kidnapping. She refuted this in a video recorded while she was still a hostage: 'The public has been told that we were irresponsible, that we were imprudent, and that therefore we are responsible for our kidnapping. That is either very cruel or very ignorant'. See 'Campaign to Free Ingrid. The Colombian FARC Delivered a Video Today in Which the Presidential Candidate Appears Alive'. Retrieved from http://web.archive.or/web/20090108020956/http://www.losverdesdeandalucia.org:80/noticia.php?id=417   (accessed 8 April 2019).

their son and a demand for a ransom of over 30,000 euros for his release. The police locate the son, but on his release they discover that the kidnapper and hostage are friends and have connived to orchestrate a hoax kidnapping. In this case the real victims are the parents, who were expected to hand over the ransom for the son and his friend to share between them.

This particular type of kidnapping is not so unusual. Every year several such cases occur and the same pattern is repeated: the kidnappers and hostages collude to obtain money (they often need fast and relatively easy access to money to settle debts), and the real victims of these hoax kidnappings are the family and friends who face pressure to pay the ransom, which according to press reports, usually ranges from 2,000 to 35,000 euros. When the security forces solve the crime, they surprise the accomplices – kidnappers and hostages – by revealing their shared secrets and responsibilities.

Such cases show the complexity of kidnapping and demonstrate the importance of carefully establishing the aspects specific to the kidnapping of democracy. Moreover, bearing in mind the primacy of political parties, governments, the mass media and trade unions in the political system, a series of doubts arise: could the victims have done more? Haven't we sometimes seen them working in cahoots with their kidnappers? Are they getting too familiar with those who hold them hostage?

Clearly each institution – political parties, the mass media and trade unions – bears different responsibilities. They are all at least partial victims insofar as they are hostages and have lost some of their freedom to act. However, it is also true that they are also partly responsible for their situation. Some institutions seem to feel quite at home under the shadow of their kidnappers and the luxuries and privileges they bring with them. Others have been unable to contain their own weaknesses and desires for power and have effectively allowed their kidnappers to exploit them. In general, trade unions have been incapable of renewing their structures, dynamics and demands in a globalized context, while the mass media have prioritized economic consolidation to the detriment of information as a counter\power; political parties have brought their programmes and ideals into disrepute by focusing on their own survival as power structures, while governments have failed in their attempts to halt the march of transnational powers. They have all allowed themselves to be seduced and trapped by power, and thus have contributed to their own captivity.

All of the above brings us to the following paradox: these institutions have fallen victim to their kidnappers' powers of seduction and to the huge challenges they have faced, especially globalization, but at the same time they are also accomplices to the crime for not having caught sight of it earlier, for not having stopped it and for not reporting it when they had the chance. That they are still doing nothing to prevent it places democracy itself in great danger.

The current state of captivity is the result of an incapacity to curb the kidnappers' power, which brings us to the final victim: the population as a whole. We will see later that there are a few exceptions and some resistance has been attempted, but the democratic institutions that purportedly represent their citizens have been taken hostage and in the end it is the general public that bears the brunt of the consequences. Citizens are asked to make sacrifices to remedy a situation they have not directly caused. Moreover, there is a further contradiction: even if the ransom is paid, there is no subsequent liberation of the hostages because the institutions, theoretically representatives of the people, are still held to ransom. The plight of citizens is, therefore, highly complex: they must endure enforced restrictions and cutbacks in a context in which their representatives no longer guarantee their interests. In the kidnapping of democracy, the hostages were party to their own captivity, a situation they will now struggle to escape from. Citizens are the direct victims of these events, and for their voices to be heard (and their votes counted), institutions must first regain their freedom. This, however, may be little more than an illusion, since the kidnappers' power hinges on the continuity of the current situation.

At this point, we now turn to the kidnappers, their identities and their methods.

6

THE KIDNAPPERS

Former FBI negotiator Gary Noesner, who was instrumental in the liberation of numerous kidnapped victims throughout his long career, claims that his work in discovering who is behind the crime is of very little relevance. In an interview with the Colombian newspaper *El Tiempo* he states that 'the key is to determine what they [those responsible] are looking for' (DIAOQU 2010). He believes that by understanding the kidnappers' reasons, a connection can be established with them that – with a strategy, patience and some luck – will lead to the hostages' release.

In the case at hand, the kidnapping of democracy, we have yet to consider the conditions necessary to negotiate a possible release of democracy and the role that negotiators might play in this endeavour, questions that are covered in later chapters (chapters 8 and 9). At this point, we can begin to explore the kidnappers' motives and briefly outline their identity, or at least their profiles and professional groups.

The first hurdle in this task is the particular nature of the kidnapping of democracy, in that it is undertaken with great stealth. The kidnappers operate behind a mask of utter normality. They do not satisfy their greed by asking for high ransoms. Indeed, the sacrifices they expect of their victims are put forward as normal requirements and, in practice, merely serve to maintain and perhaps reinforce their power and control. The false normality and lack of transparency in this process complicate the task of identifying the kidnappers. Exploring the new turns that came out of the 2008 crisis may help us advance towards our objective.

KIDNAPPING DEMOCRACY: A CRISIS OR SOMETHING ELSE?

There have been many economic and political crises throughout history, so what aspects differentiate the latest crisis from previous events? At the start of the crisis in 2008, the economist and Nobel laureate Joseph Stiglitz wrote an article titled 'The End of Neoliberalism?' Although he made no predictions, he did leave the door open to hope by stating, 'Neoliberal market fundamentalism was always a political doctrine serving certain interests. It was never supported by economic theory. Nor, it should be clear now, is it supported by historical experience. Learning this lesson may be the silver lining in the cloud now hanging over the global economy' (Stiglitz 2008).

This silver lining that Stiglitz hoped would soon materialize does not seem to have penetrated the minds of the world's key decision makers, because the economic paradigm that collapsed, or seemed to collapse at that time, has emerged unscathed and unaltered; indeed, it is now stronger and more deeply rooted than ever. Perhaps it is no exaggeration to state that the economic crisis of 2008–2009 was the catalyst that accelerated a political transformation that had been ongoing for years, and rather than reversing neoliberal market fundamentalism, it has actually cemented it. This is a salient point as major crises tend to be accompanied by obvious changes in the politicoeconomic paradigm. The durability and this potential strengthening of the predominant economic model led Colin Crouch to ask about *The Strange Non-Death of Neoliberalism* in his book, first published in 2011. Attending to the most recent past, according to Crouch, we see that the imposition of neoliberalism began when 'its opposed predecessor, generally known as Keynesian demand management, entered its own massive crisis in the inflation of the 1970s' (2011, 1). However, if this were the case in the latest crisis, and as it is not the first time that it has happened, how can we explain that neoliberal hegemony did not come to an end after the 2008–2009 crisis? How have the forces that gained the most from this system, the global corporations, managed to hold on to and even strengthen their control? And moreover, how can we explain the fortified position of the very banks that triggered the crisis?

There may be numerous explanations for this turning point resulting from the 2008 crisis, and this is what distinguishes it from previous crises. As indicated earlier, globalization is key to this explanation because, for the first time, confrontations between financial and political powers take place at a global level in a landscape where well-established transnational governmental institutions are conspicuous by their absence. Globalization is undoubtedly a significant factor, but it is also worth noting the rise of a now well-established elite, one that has successfully seized control of our democratic institutions. What is different this time is the existence of certain elites whose members come from a variety of groups that have successfully combined their interests and forces to ensure that their own privileges prevail by stealthily taking control of certain key institutions. These elites are precisely the kidnappers of democracy that we address in this book.

THE KIDNAPPED RECOGNIZE THEIR CAPTIVITY

It is striking how two leaders from opposite ends of the political spectrum, Mariano Rajoy and Yanis Varoufakis, have made similar statements about the captivity of their respective countries. In 2012, then Spanish prime minister Mariano Rajoy stated in the Spanish House of Commons that

> The Spanish have reached a point where we cannot choose between remaining as we are or making sacrifices. We do not

have that freedom. The circumstances are not so generous. Our only option in this situation is to accept that we must make sacrifices and renounce some things; or refuse to make sacrifices and renounce everything. (Parliamentary Record of the Spanish Congress of Deputies, the 10th Legislature, 2012, no. 47, p. 12. Cited in Sánchez Cuenca 2014, 20)

The former Greek finance minister Yanis Varoufakis stated during a speech given in 2015,

Why stage a coup d'état when you can send to a freshly elected government the President of the Eurogroup to tell the new finance minister, three days after taking office, that he faces a choice: the pre-existing Austerity Program, which resulted in his country's Great Depression, or the closure of the nation's banks? Why send troops in when you can have monthly Troika visits for the explicit purpose of taking over every branch of government and writing each and every piece of a nation's legislation? (Varoufakis 2015)

The tone of the two statements sets them apart, however: Rajoy appears resigned to the fact that sacrifices will have to be made, whereas Varoufakis expresses defiance and is offended by the situation. Nevertheless, the two statements reflect the belief of both a (former) prime minister and a (former) finance minister (and the citizens they represent) that they have no choice; they are not free to decide their countries' futures because they are subject to external forces that determine not only their own fate, but also that of their respective citizens. These cases reflect the situation in two southern European countries that were particularly hard hit by the economic crisis. Both are hostages of other powers, but what are those powers? Are they the same as for other countries? How can we tell the difference?

This situation is not exclusive to just one or two countries, or even a single area; the kidnapping of democracy has spread to many apparently stable and well-established Western democracies. Although each situation has its own hostages and victims, and responsible parties, they are not the same in each context. The kidnappers tailor their activities and strategies to the conditions in each specific country. They are not the same in Spain as they are in the United States or Australia, which makes them even more difficult to identify, but their presence is felt in many liberal democracies and their power is on the rise.

MASTERS OF MANKIND

Democracy is being kidnapped by certain elite groups that have taken over the basic institutions of the democratic system. In the eighteenth century, the pioneering political economist and philosopher Adam Smith (Conill 2006) wrote about what he called 'the masters of mankind', whom he identified as the traders and manufacturers in Great Britain at that time, characterized by their 'rapacity' and 'monopolizing spirit' (Smith 2007 [1776], 380). Although a defender of the free market, Smith argued that these nuclei of economic power must at all costs be prevented from establishing monopolies and shifting their power to the political domain, because this would also turn them into 'the rulers of mankind' (Smith, 2007). This is precisely what has happened today: the economic powers have colonized political power. Yesterday's 'masters of mankind' are today's elites and, more specific, today's financial oligarchies. They have very efficiently extended their control to other areas of representative democracies, which has consolidated the kidnapping.

Several contemporary works can help us understand who these new governors are and their modus operandi. Some key titles are *L'Hydre Mondiale. L'Oligopole Bancaire* (*The World Hydra, the Bank Oligopoly*), by François Morin; *The Never Ending Nightmare*, by Pierre Dardot and Christian Laval; *The Strange Non-Death of Neoliberalism*, by Colin Crouch or *La impotencia democrática*, by Ignacio Sánchez-Cuenca, among many others.

Today's oligarchies owe their newfound strength to the convergence and coalition of various powerful groups whose common interests and projects have led them to join forces. They share the idea that stability and general development is guaranteed by concentrating resources and wealth in just a few hands (especially their own). This elite group has consolidated an extensive network of influences, bringing together big names in the world's economy that share the same worldview. They include multinational corporations from the arms, pharmaceutical and energy sectors, among others, but it is the banking sector that leads the race to control the political sphere in existing democracies, with the invaluable collaboration of the oligopoly of the main rating agencies.

In his *L'Hydre Mondiale. L'Oligopole Bancaire* (*The World Hydra, the Bank Oligopoly*), economist François Morin argues that it is the World Bank and specifically the twenty-eight large international banks that have recently crushed and overpowered democracy. Not only do these banks influence and define the financial sector, they also act as a highly organized unified group capable of imposing regulations and amending policies. Morin demonstrates that these banks are of such magnitude and importance that their resources exceed the public debt of dozens of countries, a fortune that gives them enormous power and, in turn, allows us to contextualize the events that followed the great crisis of 2008–2009. At the time of the financial crash, the big banks held vast quantities of toxic products and much of the responsibility for the fatal economic aftermath can be laid at their feet. Yet rather than paying for these consequences, they convinced national governments to bail them out. Remarkably, during this bail-out process, the rules of the game remained the same, and the repercussions of these political measures did not fall on those that triggered the crisis, at least not as severely. The banking world was simply too big and too powerful to fail and was therefore bailed out with taxpayers' money, and private debt became public debt. Taxpayers paid the ransom, yet governments were not freed by their captors. Indeed, quite the opposite occurred: the kidnappers imposed their rationale and their power was strengthened.

Apart from the big banks, other key institutions played their part in the kidnapping. The International Monetary Fund (IMF), created in 1944 to – in theory – secure economic stability, and the European Central Bank (ECB), whose noble intention is to maintain price stability in the Eurozone, now act as mediators between the financial system and governments, but with a clear remit to prioritize the interests of the financial system. Logically, the troika, comprising the IMF, the ECB and the European Commission, also falls into this group.

FROM THE LOBBY INTO THE CHAMBER

Numerous groups with multiple interests can be found in a democratic society and mediating among them is a political task. Naturally, as part of this democratic mediation process, diverse interest groups attempt to influence their representatives in their political decision making. Known as lobbies, these pressure groups date back to the eighteenth century in the British Parliament and aim to persuade politicians to make decisions in favour of their particular interests. Lobbying is often a hotly debated issue as it can unbalance the representation of interests in society. However, this debate becomes a matter of urgency when lobbyists operate without transparency or clear regulations.

What is happening in the current kidnapping of democracy goes beyond this process. The term *lobbying* derives from the hallways where British members of parliament assemble before parliamentary debates and, as Crouch reminds us, its political use refers to the influence exerted by pressure groups in this particular place (2011). These groups aimed to make their demands heard before their elected representatives entered the chamber where final decision making took place. The entrance to the chamber was reserved exclusively for representatives of the population.

The strategies adopted by pressure groups to persuade representatives in the lobby are diverse, and some are more desirable than others. However, the current problem is not only the increasingly aggressive methods lobbyists adopt to persuade representatives, but the elimination of the door separating the lobby from the chamber. Today's oligarchies no longer wait in the lobby to meet passing representatives; rather, they are in the room where decisions are made. Crouch describes how they act as government consultants: they have their own people attached to ministers' offices, they make regulations, 'mediate' in shaping governments and so on (Crouch 2011). In sum, not only do they influence, but they also at times impose decisions on those who purportedly represent the electorate.

SOME OF THE KIDNAPPERS' METHODS

The kidnappers employ a wide range of methods. Notwithstanding, some strategies are used with particular insistence and efficiency, such as blackmail or hiring certain people for key positions, popularly known as the revolving door phenomenon.

Blackmail can take various forms and is spread through several different channels. Large multinational firms employ this strategy when they relocate production to other countries by demanding tax advantages and subsidies, or asking for certain regulations to be waived. Indeed, relocation negotiations never take place in conditions of equality; the playing field always slopes in favour of the multinational and not the country's political authorities. Large corporations also use blackmail as a direct strategy in their dealings with political parties and elected representatives; one example is party funding. In countries like the United States, fundraising for candidates during electoral campaigns is big business. Because a candidate's fate is often determined by how much money they raise, it is hardly surprising that large companies take advantage of this to further their own interests. In Europe, particularly in the south, blackmailing has also left its mark on some states' politics; the Greek case is the most paradigmatic – and cruellest – of them all. In 2011, Georgios Papandreu, at that time the prime minister of Greece, was forced to resign after proposing a referendum on the structural adjustment programme imposed on Greece by the troika. He was replaced by an insider from the banking sector, Lucas Papademos, who had until then held the position of governor of the Central Greek Bank. When SYRIZA came to power in 2015, winning the elections with a clear anti-austerity programme, the troika and the rating agencies set in motion a fierce blackmail strategy. The new government, led by Alexis Tsipras, was subjected to a veritable demonstration of power, which Dardot and Laval called 'debtocracy'. This method implies that the national politics of a country is directed from outside to ensure that they do not make the 'wrong' decisions. Any government that challenges this orthodoxy will, as Dardor and Laval state, be immediately punished by having loan requests refused or their ratings lowered by the credit agencies, which ipso facto raises the interest rates due to creditors (2019). Some debtor countries, like Greece, Ireland or Cyprus, have experienced this treatment first hand, while others have 'promoted' technocratic governments (such as that of Mario Monti in Italy between 2011 and 2013). The electoral promises made by certain political parties have little chance of coming to fruition because of the coercion they are likely to face from creditors and rating agencies. Parties and governments are mere hostages in this all too frequent blackmail strategy.

As well as blackmail, kidnappers also apply strategies such as the so-called revolving door practice. This strategy favours a peculiar symbiosis by rotating positions in large multinational firms (particularly in the finance sector) and high-level public positions in national and transnational political institutions, and is not associated with any particular country. This 'special' relationship may guarantee obvious benefits for those taking part, but it is far from clear that it is useful for democracy and for the independence of its institutions. The proliferation of such cases is driven by an intention to establish relationships that blur the division between politics and the economy in favour of the latter. Dardot and Laval have examined this phenomenon in the French context, where there is a conspicuous association between the banking world and the public administration. Other authors such as Luis Miguel Montero have uncovered many such cases in Spain, which is riddled with examples of large IBEX 35 companies hiring former political representatives (Montero 2016). This is now relatively common practice and certain flagrant cases spring to mind of individuals switching from the political to the financial domain (Otmar Issing, Felipe González, Rodrigo Rato, José María Aznar, to name just a few), or in the opposite direction from finance to politics (Mario Draghi, Mario Monti, Mark Carney, Romano Prodi, Lukas Papademus and many more).

Blackmail and revolving doors are two of the main strategies used to carry out a kidnapping and override institutions' political capacity, thereby blurring the boundaries between political and economic powers to the detriment of the citizens who suffer the consequences. Political pluralism is thus removed, and the representative role of political parties and governments is called into question. So as Sánchez-Cuenca states, 'if we knew beforehand that whichever party wins, regardless of its ideology, it would be obliged to implement 'sacrifices', then why bother voting at all?' (2014, 20). Democracy is clearly emptied of content whenever citizen preferences no longer guide political decisions but are replaced with those of others – banks, multinational firms from all sectors, rating agencies or supranational institutions with no democratic basis – as they impose measures in key issues and areas like the economy. This process clearly threatens the notion of self-government based on the representation of plural interests.

As previously indicated, kidnapping has also spread to other vital institutions such as the mass media and the trade unions. Some are co-opted in order to lend legitimacy to the kidnappers' political discourse through mantras such as the impossibility of adopting alternative policies, having to make sacrifices, citizens – especially from certain 'irresponsible' countries – are directly responsible for the economic crisis, and so on. Others (trade unions) are discredited or are pushed aside when real decisions have to be made.

In short, politics is handcuffed by an elite few and by certain institutions that know how to use their networks and influences to remain in power and to stealthily impose their own policies and interests. Ordinary citizens pay the final price in this process. What, therefore, is the public's response to its state of captivity?

7

VICTIMS' RESPONSE

From Stockholm Syndrome to Defiance

Each victim responds differently to being kidnapped, but the most curious and surprising reaction is the so-called Stockholm syndrome. This phenomenon first appeared in 1973 when Jan-Erik Olsson held four people hostage for six days in the Swedish capital, Stockholm. One of the hostages, Kristin Enmark, adopted the role of spokesperson for the four hostages and openly expressed sympathy for her kidnapper. Psychiatrist Nils Bejerot, who acted as a negotiator and counsellor during the kidnapping, verified this unusual reaction and coined the term *Stockholm syndrome*. Only one year later, in 1974, Patricia Hearst, the daughter of tycoon William Randolph Hearst, was kidnapped by the Symbionese Liberation Army. Weeks after her captivity (once her relations had paid a ransom), she joined the group that had illegally held her. Patricia Hearst changed her name to Tania and was photographed shortly afterwards using an assault rifle to hold up the Hibernia bank. During her trial, her lawyer used the concept of Stockholm syndrome in her defence, which brought the term into more general use.

Nearly fifty years later, this psychological response no longer surprises and is used to identify situations in which a hostage establishes an affective bond with his or her captors and may assume and accept the kidnappers' ideas, beliefs and justifications. In our analysis, we now ask whether Stockholm syndrome might be applicable to the case of the hostages and victims of a kidnapped democracy; do they show any signs of Stockholm syndrome or, conversely, do they confront their kidnappers? In this chapter, we reflect on both these possibilities, but before doing so, we first examine some of the direct consequences experienced by kidnapping victims in an attempt to contextualize the different types of reactions that take place.

THE ILLS OF KIDNAPPING

The title of the 2014 Oxfam International report *Working for the Few: Political Capture and Economic Inequality* (Fuentes-Nieva and Galasso 2014; see also Hardoon 2015) perfectly summarizes another or perhaps *the* direct consequence of a kidnapped political system: growing inequality. When political institutions fall to powerful captors, the effects will be felt both politically and economically. The severe economic crisis of 2008 and the policies implemented as a result have increased the divide between rich and poor across the globe, as evidenced in recent reports such as the *Global Wealth Report 2017* published by the Credit Suisse Bank Research Institute. The Oxfam report highlights some worrying data, such as 'eighty-five people had the same wealth as the bottom half of the world's population' (Fuentes-Nieva and Galasso 2014, 2). Similarly, the 2017 Credit Suisse report states that following the 2008 crisis, the share held by the wealthiest 1 percent rose from 42.5 percent of all household wealth to 50.1 percent in 2017 (Frank 2017).

These alarming data reflect a clear trend: the pervasive widening of the inequality gap since 2008 due to the concentration of wealth in the hands of the richest and most powerful groups. The Oxfam report *An Economy for the 1 percent* (2016) provides the following evidence for this trend: 'In 2015, just sixty-two individuals had the same wealth as 3.6 billion people – the bottom half of humanity' (Hardoon, Fuentes-Nieva and Ayele 2016, 2). In 2010, this same wealth was held by 388 people. Moreover, the wealth of the richest people increased by 45 percent in barely five years.[1] Conversely, the wealth of 'the bottom half fell by just over a trillion dollars in the same period – a drop of 38 percent' (Hardoon, Fuentes-Nieva and Ayele 2016, 2). It therefore comes as no surprise that the political slogan of the Occupy Wall Street movement, 'We are the 99 percent', has been widely embraced to denounce the present reality. In fact, a closer look at the wealth distribution index published by Credit Suisse reveals that the figure of 99 percent is actually higher, since wealth in excess of 1 million US dollars is held by 36 million individuals. This might initially seem like a large number, but it accounts for only 0.7 percent (not 1 percent) of the world's population. Moreover, claims have been made that the extremely wealthy and powerful super-rich class makes up even less than 0.1 percent, and these are the people who actually control the economy and, as we have seen, politics.

Apart from the possible debate about the exact percentage of people (predominantly white men, needless to say) who form the world's economic elite, we now know that the policies introduced in the wake of the 2008 crisis have reinforced their power and control. The sacrifices required of the general population have left deep scars, but not everyone has been affected. These policies have allowed some to benefit considerably from the crisis. The mechanisms and stratagems used to successfully consolidate and embed inequality are manifold and wide-ranging. One that has recently attracted a great deal of attention is the use of tax havens – territories or states with extremely lax tax systems that encourage large fortunes and companies to register their capital there to avoid paying tax in their own countries.

---

1. Except for South Korea, levels of inequality are rising in all high-income G20 countries.

Access to such havens and preferential tax policies in certain countries have attracted much criticism. Even multimillionaire Warren Buffett complained that 'the taxation system has tilted towards the rich and away from the middle class in the last ten years' (Clark 2007). He also considers it conspicuous that ' there wasn't anyone in the office, from the receptionist up, who paid as low a tax rate and I have no tax planning; I don't have an accountant or use tax shelters. I just follow what the US Congress tells me to do' (Clark 2007; see also Isidore 2013).

Yet because democracy has been kidnapped, the political measures required to put an end to this practice are automatically blocked by the oligarchies that use their power to protect their interests. Thus, while the policies of austerity and economic restrictions are imposed on the vast majority of the population, one small sector is left practically unscathed by these measures. In other words, not everyone has been forced to 'tighten their belt' in the same way. It is striking (although perhaps not, in light of the hijacking of democracy) that during a time of cutbacks some measures or approaches were suggested and won a certain amount of popular approval, but failed to make progress in any parliament. Such measures included a low tax on financial transactions (known as the Tobin tax after the economist James Tobin who proposed the idea), ending tax havens, raising tax slightly on large fortunes or setting a maximum salary for top executives.

Although these measures may not remove the problem of inequality, they might go some way to bridging the gap between rich and poor. What is striking and relevant, however, is that such policies are never even seriously discussed in the representative arena and, therefore, they can never actually be put into practice. The question of how to share the burden generated by the recent crisis apparently failed to penetrate either the current economic 'orthodoxy' or the decision-making process. The culture and direction of politics seem to be set in stone; anything that does not fit with this orthodoxy, determined by the oligarchies, is regarded as odd, populist, demagogic, radical, antisystem and unreal, or any other adjective that clearly denotes that there is, and can only be, one way of doing things.

VICTIMS' REACTIONS

The rise of entrenched inequality and the lack of any political will or policies to end it have not gone unnoticed by the general public. Opinion surveys such as Eurobarometer and Latinobarómetro clearly reflect public anger and discontent with the current situation. A survey conducted in 2014 by Oxfam in six different countries (Spain, South Africa, India, the UK, Brazil and the United States) found that the vast majority of the population believes that today's laws and regulations are conceived to benefit the wealthy.[2] In Europe, Eurobarometer data reveal that 45 percent of European citizens are dissatisfied with their own national democracies, while in countries like Spain this figure rises to 60 percent (Eurobarometer 2016).

In general, we now know that although the ideals and values of democracy are not refuted – indeed they are broadly welcomed and accepted – there is a widespread growing discontent with what it provides and how it functions (Galli 2013; Ganuza and Font 2018). This discontent may well be explained, at least in part, by the crime we are dealing with here: kidnapping. It is therefore appropriate to now observe some of the ways citizens are reacting to their growing discontent. We should not forget that citizens still have control at the ballot box and that they are the ones directly suffering the consequences of this hijacking of democracy. Levels of discontent are reaching such a decisive point as to suggest that the extreme reaction described in Saramago's novel *Seeing* could actually become a feasible reality in the short or long term. However, election results show that current levels of anger, outrage and discontent have not led to major popular 'revolts' of this kind, at least in the polls, although voters' preferences are becoming

---

2. According to this report, more than 80 percent of people in Spain think this way.

more volatile. So what are the most notable reactions to the results of our kidnapped democracies?

The Electoral Stockholm Syndrome

In a 2003 *New York Times* article, journalist David Brooks asked the question, 'Why don't people vote their own self-interest?' and went on to provide an illustrative example relating to US politics. Brooks described how, in the United States, the Republican Party periodically proposes a series of tax cuts that are actually only designed to benefit the top 1 percent of the country's wealthiest citizens. In turn, the Democratic Party denounces these schemes every time they are presented. Yet they are always approved (with some minor amendments) by the legislative power and, as Al Gore's 2000 campaign clearly showed, the Democrats are incapable of obtaining sufficient electoral support to detain them.[3] Brooks then wonders why people do not wholeheartedly support proposals that could benefit them personally. Why do the people who most suffer from certain policies end up supporting them? Or, going a stage further, why are there not more revolts against such blatantly unfair situations?

Brooks states that there are many reasons for this, but both the perception of one's own condition and the hope of climbing up the social ladder play a key role in the search for answers. He reminds us that during the 2000 campaign, *Time* magazine conducted a survey that asked people if they were part of the top 1 percent of earners. The results revealed that 19 percent considered themselves to be, while another 20 percent expected to be part of it one day. In other words, 39 percent of the surveyed population felt that Al Gore was directly attacking them by criticizing plans that would exclusively benefit the 1 percent.

Studies on system justification theory find that even more aspects intervene in this process (Jost, Banaji and Nosek 2004). It is

---

3. This article is cited in the work by Jost, Banaji and Nosek (2004). Original text Brooks (2003).

commonly believed that citizens can easily be manipulated by the persuasive messages in the mass media. We also now know that these media (and their owners) use various strategies to maintain and secure the status quo (as we saw in chapter 3). Using fear through strategies like the shock doctrine, as Naomi Klein claims, is a good example of the way the elites efficiently control citizens (Klein 2007). Yet these theories explain only a part of the story; internal psychological factors also intervene and act to contextualize the reasons why there are not more revolts against injustices. Howard Zinn tells us to bear in mind what has happened throughout history:

> Society's tendency is to maintain what has been. Rebellion is only an occasional reaction to suffering in human history; we have infinitely more instances of forbearance to exploitation, and submission to authority, than we have examples of revolt. Measure the number of peasant insurrections against the centuries of serfdom in Europe—the millennia of landlordism in the East; match the number of slave revolts in America with the record of those millions who went through their lifetimes of toil without outward protest. What we should be most concerned about is not some natural tendency towards violent uprising, but rather the inclination of people, faced with an overwhelming environment, to submit to it. (Zinn 1968, 16–17. Cited in Jost, Banaji and Nosek 2004, 886)

System justification theory shows us that individuals have a certain tendency to rationalize the status quo by perceiving it as natural, legitimate and acceptable (Jost and Kay 2005; Jost, Banaji and Nosek 2004). Not only do we see ourselves as being above our 'real' position and aspire to climb higher, but we also rationalize the situation in which we are destined to live. In addition, approaches such as cognitive dissonance theory hold that the most disadvantaged individuals with the fewest resources are those that develop the greatest need to justify their own suffering as a way of reducing their internal discord. In other words, it is precisely those who suffer the most that need to rationalize and justify their own situation to mitigate the psychological stress brought on by living in these circumstances (Lane 2004; Jost et al. 2003).

Social psychology continues to explore these questions in what remains an open debate. However, it seems clear that certain internal personality factors influence our acceptance of inequality and injustices. As Jost, Banaji and Nosek state, we cannot rule out the possibility 'that human beings have developed generally adaptive capacities to accommodate, internalize, and even rationalize key features of their socially constructed environments, especially those features that are difficult or impossible to change' (2004, 912). These adaptive capacities have an enormous repercussion that we simply cannot ignore or set aside in our reflection because it implies that, although we are unaware of it, the status quo holds enormous power over us.

At this point we must return to our story since these reflections may throw some light on recent election results, which reflect widespread citizen discontent across the globe. Many studies have examined the decline of certain political parties in the past years, finding a particular loss of support for some social democratic parties in Europe. Recent elections in countries like France, the Netherlands, Greece and Italy (Welp 2018) offer some examples, although other political parties have also experienced a significant loss of voters. Notwithstanding, less attention has been paid to the opposite trend, namely, the staying power of conventional or traditional political parties, despite enormous voter disaffection. It is worth remembering that high percentages of the population (up to 80 percent of those surveyed) in some contexts often state that political parties 'are only concerned about their own electoral interests', 'do not represent the voice of the people', 'do not promote the best people in their party structures', 'are corrupt' or 'offer no really alternative programmes and proposals'. Although such concerns are expressed differently in every context, they are repeated in the results of public opinion surveys conducted in very diverse countries. Despite this, election results also indicate that conventional political parties are still holding their ground. It is true that voting volatility does exist (we reflect on this in the next point), as do cases of parties on the wane, but electoral outcomes show that in general, mainstream parties are still in good health. In fact, voter behaviour analysis would conclude that a significant section of the electorate maintains its support for the electoral forces with which it has clearly expressed its anger or disaffection. That is, people continue voting for the same parties despite their anger over the way politicians justify the cuts to public services that personally affect them, play down cases of corruption or defend policies that strengthen the power of the oligarchies.

This is a complex matter to grasp. Moreover, but no less important, we must remember that this particular relationship with political parties is linked to another key aspect, namely, how citizens perceive the crisis. It is useful to look at southern Europe again. Following the collapse of the economy, blame was assigned to the general public. A series of themes ('frames' or 'metaphors', see Lakoff 2014) gradually appeared, suggesting that the crisis was not due to bad praxis or abuse of power but to 'irresponsible' citizens who had 'lived well above their means'. Because citizens had behaved irresponsibly (especially those in southern Europe) and had clearly caused the crisis, they would have to pay the cost through public spending cuts, for example. Certain political parties were behind these accusations, which were reproduced unchallenged in much of the media. Most striking, and perhaps most worrying, these messages have gotten through to the public since, as several sociological studies have shown, citizens have assumed and internalized the thesis of their own responsibility for triggering the crisis (Alonso et al. 2017; Ganuza and Font 2018). Many people blame themselves for the crisis, and they believe that their purchasing decisions were just as much to blame for the economic-financial collapse as the elites who had promoted economic models based on speculation (Alonso and Fernández-Rodríguez 2018). We can therefore see how the Stockholm syndrome has also made its presence felt here, at a time when some sections of society accept the justifications of the promoters or collaborators in the kidnapping of democratic institutions. Victims feel guilty for their situation and they have internalized the explanations given to

them about the origin of the crisis, as well as the purported 'necessary' measures to deal with it. They are the ones actually suffering
the consequences, but they justify the actions of the kidnappers
and their accomplices by incorporating their metaphors and ra-
tionalizing the established status quo.

Electoral 'Rebelliousness'

Returning to the question of citizens' reactions in the electoral
domain, another trend is what we might term rebellious voter
syndrome. This refers to the reaction of voters who, in the knowledge that they have been taken hostage and that political parties'
hands are tied because of pressure from economic-financial
forces, seek an alternative to traditional political parties, or at least
express their anger in the polls through more imaginative means.
This search for an alternative could have very different and unpredictable outcomes both in terms of the type of (new) party they
may support and their attitude to elections, which might include
abstaining, casting a blank ballot or spoiling their ballot paper.
This growing reaction corresponds to an attitude of protest that
reflects a certain weariness and frustration with the more established parties.

The international spread of parties labelled as populist but with
highly divergent ideologies and success rates at the polls might be
associated with the consolidation of the 'rebellious voter'. Many
analysts believe that the electoral success of such parties is due to
their populist leaders' communication skills and the use of emotional strategies in their election campaigns. So, depending on the
analytical interpretation, the success of these politicians lies in
their communication skills and their capacity to persuade less intelligent voters to choose the 'wrong way' and to support 'danger-
ous' (antisystem) populist parties. The effective communication
strategies of these parties may indeed have a strong influence;
however, it may also be the case that this type of analysis mista-
kenly identifies the causes of their electoral success. It is also

simplistic to consider all those who vote for these parties as less intelligent.

A significant segment of the electorate seems to be expressing something different. They think their voices are not heard and they doubt that mainstream parties can truly represent their interests. They prefer to believe that there is little difference between the parties and their programmes, and in any case, politicians prioritize other interests and respond to pressure from other spheres. These voters have no faith that their vote for one of the traditional A, B or C options will have any effect and, driven by their frustration, weariness or their desire for change, end up voting for Z (or spoil their paper, cast a blank vote or abstain).

The intention of some of these voters is to put pressure on or force a reaction from the mainstream parties; others want to express their discontent, and yet others place their hopes in new parties being able to represent interests that escape the control of the elites. In 2016 the economist and journalist Martin Wolf wrote in an article published in the *Financial Times* that many voters consider themselves to be the real losers of the economic crisis and believe that their vote may at least express their revolt against the elites (Wolf 2016). Wolf is probably right. Rebellious voters want freedom from their captivity, so they use their vote imaginatively by changing their traditional electoral behaviour, a situation that is currently giving more than one headache to statistics buffs and electoral poll designers. Some voters are aware of the problems described in this book: that representatives and political parties, together with the other institutions mentioned in chapters 2, 3 and 4, are tied by external forces and do not carry out the main task assigned to them in the democratic system, which is to represent the plural interests of society. The rebellious voter does not give too much importance to which party – conservative or progressive – wins the election because whatever the case, decisions are taken in another sphere or at another level. This would also explain the recent pronounced volatility in voters' opinions.

In short, this chapter has uncovered two possible symptoms that, while certainly not the only dynamics affecting voting trends, are beginning to spread. I am not saying that all those who vote for a new party are automatically rebellious voters, nor that anyone who decides to support a mainstream party is a victim of Stockholm syndrome. This categorization does not focus on the outcome (who they vote for) but on the reason that leads voters to pick one option or another. Assimilating the discourse of captors and accomplices brings us closer to the Stockholm syndrome voter, whereas a decision based on anger, frustration and protest is what differentiates a rebellious voter.

Voters who experience one of these syndromes have different responses to kidnapping. The Stockholm syndrome voters seem to have internalized their captors' narrative, or accept their state of captivity, or trust that the mainstream parties will find a way to get the situation back on track and regain the legitimacy they once had as the go-betweens and representatives of wide-ranging plural interests. The rebellious voters, in turn, want to express their anger at the ballet box and perhaps even use their vote to bring about change by trusting new parties (or representatives) to drive this transformation. In the first scenario, we might find that mainstream parties are unable, or unwilling, to recover their sovereignty and the capacity to face up to the kidnappers. In the second scenario, new parties may bring about a real fruitful change, or they might fail in their attempt and quickly become no different from the mainstream political parties. Or they may simply turn out to be imposters with allegiances to the elites or, in some cases, their seductive electoral tactics are just masking old formulas. Whatever the case, the question of how we can free democracy from its captivity is the subject of the final chapter of this book; but first we must ask where the negotiators are, because no kidnapping takes place without an attempt to resolve it.

8

NEGOTIATORS

One actor that can have a crucial role in a kidnapping is the negotiator. The tension of the kidnapping requires the involvement of professionals capable of dealing with and solving the situation. Negotiators deal directly with the people responsible for the crime, and their mission is to ensure the well-being and interests of hostages and victims. They need excellent communication skills and intelligence to anticipate the kidnappers' moves. Teams of negotiators normally operate in groups, some investigating the crime and others communicating with the captors. Their profiles may vary, but members of special kidnapping units tend to have communication and emotional self-control skills and high levels of empathy and creativity. Negotiators identify their most critical skills as a keen ability to listen and an eye for decisive details. The negotiator's work is highly complex because of the tension involved and the potential duration of the kidnapping. The situation might last for days or even weeks, and negotiators are likely to form close relationships with the hostages and their families, as well as with the kidnappers. The negotiator's role is pivotal in securing the hostage's release, and while success cannot be guaranteed, there is a greater likelihood of a happy ending when these professionals are involved.

At this point we should ask whether anyone is negotiating the terms on which the kidnappers of democracy might surrender or attempting to defend citizens' interests. We have already seen that the kidnapping of democracy has certain unique characteristics. It is a stealthy operation because the captors' intention is to prolong and maintain the situation over time. They subtly impose their claims and interests without noisily drawing attention. What they essentially aspire to is a silent protracted kidnapping.

Moreover, the hostages – political parties, governments, trade unions and the mass media – have been captured as a result of their own internal weaknesses and the kidnappers' powers of seduction. As the key actors in the political system, they are generally seen to be colluding with events because their privileges remain unthreatened. Moreover, whenever these privileges are challenged, their survival instincts drive them back into the comfortable arms of their kidnappers.

Citizens are, therefore, the victims of a kidnapped democracy: the institutions and professionals that should be acting as negotiators and representing them have capitulated. It is precisely the hostages described in this book (especially the political parties) that we would have expected to act as negotiators. Moreover, they have set themselves up as accomplices in the kidnapping. In a situation of political 'normality' in which all democratic institutions are free, they are supposed to be skilled listeners and have the capacity to mediate among diverse social groups. At the same time, we would also expect these institutions to be capable of developing intelligent efficient strategies to protect the political system against potential threats of takeover or blackmail from economic powers, in order to guarantee its continued smooth operations.

However, it seems as though citizens cannot expect a heroic negotiator to come to the rescue and return democracy and its institutions to its "free" state any time soon. As a result, the present chapter is inevitably very brief and, as I have attempted to show throughout this book, those in spheres of power that could potentially take on the role of negotiator and go-between are locked up in captivity. A few isolated voices have sounded the alarm, and social movements and NGOs are doing what they can to mount resistance. There are also some signs of resistance from a few prominent hostages. Notwithstanding, the balance is clearly tipped in the kidnappers' favour since their disproportionate power appears to be unthreatened. The entrenchment of this danger and the realization that we cannot wait for a negotiator to step in leads us to reflect on alternative strategies to secure the release of democracy, the subject of the final chapter.

9

THE STRUGGLE FOR LIBERATION

The kidnapping of individuals is a temporary circumstance in which securing the release of the hostages is the chief objective for the authorities, as well as for the hostages themselves. Success is far from guaranteed, since this particular crime generates great tension and puts the hostages' lives in danger, and indeed, many cases have ended in tragedy. When attempting to liberate the hostages the authorities and security forces have to deal with diverse scenarios and employ a range of strategies. Although saving the lives of the hostages is paramount, there are several ways in which this can be achieved.

One solution is to give in to the kidnappers by paying the ransom or satisfying their demands, and then waiting for them to release the hostages safely. This is usually considered as the last option because it can encourage the spread of such crimes. In other situations, the crime may be resolved if the kidnappers can be persuaded to surrender and release the hostages. This was the case of the unusual hijacking of the Libyan Afriqiyah Airways plane that was forced to land on the island of Malta in December 2016. Two men, apparently promoting a new Libyan political platform loyal to the overthrown dictator Muammar Gaddafi, held 109 passengers and six crew members hostage but eventually surrendered peacefully following negotiations. In other cases, investigators locate the whereabouts of the hostages and proceed to release them. In Spain, the kidnapping of José Antonio Ortega Lara by the ETA terrorist group ended after 532 days once the security forces had learned he was being held in an underground dungeon in an industrial warehouse by tracing a previously intercepted note to an ETA leader. This note contained the information 'Ortega 5K' followed by 'BOL', which first identified José Manuel Uribetxeberria Bolinaga as responsible for the kidnapping and shortly thereafter enabled the discovery of Ortega Lara's whereabouts in July 1997.

Other highly complex rescue operations have also been mounted. One of the operations most widely covered in the media was Operation Jaque. This took place in Colombia with the participation of the military forces, who infiltrated the FARC (Revolutionary Armed Forces of Colombia – People's Army) to release fifteen hostages, including Ingrid Betancourt. In the final phase of this operation, the military forces convinced two FARC leaders to transfer the hostages using an army-owned helicopter with a military crew, which was presented to the FARC as belonging to an NGO. Once the helicopter took off the two leaders were captured and the hostages were released.

BACK TO THE IDIOSYNCRASIES OF AN ABDUCTED DEMOCRACY

The kidnapping of democracy has unique features that must be kept in mind when considering methods of liberation. Observing the processes used in conventional kidnappings allows us to at least rule out the most unsuitable options. For example, a negotiation process followed by the kidnappers' voluntary surrender would seem fairly implausible: first, because the chances of a negotiator being involved are very slim, and second, because the kidnappers are highly unlikely to relinquish their hold during negotiations.

Neither does paying a ransom in exchange for the liberation of democratic institutions appear to be an appropriate strategy. The captors have no intention of handing over the precious assets in their control; on the contrary, their aim is to prolong the captivity of democracy in perpetuity and by any means possible because this is their main source of privilege, lifestyle and socioeconomic security. In the event that the kidnappers request or force a ransom, it will not be to relinquish their control over democracy but to reinforce it.

However, determining the whereabouts of the hostages, as in the Ortega Lara case, can advance the task we propose here. Yet as we have already established that the kidnapping of democracy involves multiple hostages and victims, perhaps the key lies less in locating them than in their release. Although it is important to identify and locate the hostages and any other victims, it is also necessary to expand the range of strategies or methods to secure their liberation. We must remember that these are extremely secretive hijackings in which appearances and forms are kept up to give a semblance of normality in which both institutions and citizens are (or appear to be) totally at liberty.

If we accept that these options are unviable, and that a Jaque-style rescue operation of democracy is little more than a fantasy, the solutions and strategies remaining to us are extremely limited, particularly when confronted by a complex situation requiring a far from simple solution. Indeed, at this point I must confess that I have no concrete solutions to the enormous problem facing us. I do not have enough knowledge at my disposal to write a *Democracy Liberation Manual* containing the necessary guidelines to complete this task with any guarantee of success. This project also requires a very broad, long-term and profound reflection that goes well beyond the scope of these few pages and would be another project of greater magnitude.

Notwithstanding, we must not be discouraged by this problem or resign ourselves to it, just as we cannot abandon this book without addressing the final phase. Liberation may require a series of interconnected strategies to trigger the dismantling of the power structures that the kidnappers will undoubtedly fight to prevent. However, we must also consider that we have an advantage since the groundwork for these strategies has already been laid: resistance based on mobilizations and the development of proposals and participatory experiments are working to free democracy from its captivity. In this final chapter we will examine some of the most notable examples, but first we revisit the meaning of democracy and its possibilities.

RETHINKING DEMOCRACY

The prevailing model of democracy today is, as noted in chapter 2, that of representative-electoral democracy. This format predominated when a system based on the 'power of the *demos* ' was put into practice. In this model, citizens' participatory capacity is primarily defined through voting, while the work of the rulers is to interpret and represent the people's needs, interests and preferences. However, this is only one specific form of democracy. Other conceptions and visions of the democratic system complement or even differ from the representative model, on the understanding that citizen participation cannot be based solely on casting a vote in the ballot box every so often.

In this vein, we now have proposals and models of democracy that recognize the need to strengthen the processes of deliberation in decision making or the configuration of the political agenda, either in areas linked to governmental institutions or in areas of civil society (Habermas 1996; Fishkin 2011). Other proposals advocate that as well as voting, citizens should also implement processes to follow up and monitor representative institutions and their actors so they are in a position to sound the alarm in the event of failure or abuse of power, in order to put in motion a purge of responsibilities and ensure enhanced political procedures (Keane 2009). Other democratic models go a step further by insisting on numerous mechanisms of direct participation in which citizens can collectively decide their future (Barber 2003). All these proposals, despite their obvious differences, share a common basic idea: the need to expand the meaning and possibilities of citizen participation.

In recent years we have witnessed a spread of this demand for extended citizen participation beyond the bounds of political theories with civil society movements claiming to espouse 'true democracy' or 'real democracy' in many parts of the world. Today, the principal structures of representative democracy have been taken captive by other powers. Representative democracy is a proposal of minimums in terms of demanding and understanding citizen participation, but that seems to be a long way from the modus operandi intended by authors such as Schumpeter, Sartori, Dahl and others. Their institutions are not free, and hence, not even the vote (a participation mechanism that by its very nature is already limited) has a decisive and profound impact on the future of political life. Negotiators of interests and preferences (governments, parties and unions especially) under the control of other powers cannot exercise their negotiating power, and citizens lose even their indirect influence on decisions that affect them in a very direct way. The representative democracy model concentrates decision making (and political power) in a relatively small number of institutions and people, which smooths its implementation in complex and heavily populated societies such as ours. However, entrusting decision making to a small group of governors also makes the system more vulnerable to certain sectors (such as the economic sector), which then both influence and dominate the political sphere through the strategies described in chapter 6. It is therefore not surprising that more direct models of democracy are pressing for the urgent expansion of citizen participation, since this would favour a greater distribution of responsibilities and power, which in turn would impede the colonization of politics by other powers. These proposals can help shed some light on strategies that are currently being developed and that perhaps can be used to drive the liberation of democracy.

THE ACCOMPLICES . . .
ARE THEY STIRRING FROM THEIR LETHARGY?

A key step for the liberation of democracy would be to prevent institutions and the people in them from acting as accomplices. That is, the structures understood to be the pillars of the representative democratic system should be able to function independently and act as mediators of the plural interests of society. A further useful step would be for these institutions (especially governments and political parties) to open up new channels of communication and participation with society. This proposed form of action to consolidate a truly representative democratic model would incorporate complementary citizen participation mechanisms.

We have previously reflected on a group of actors who play a paradoxical role in the abduction of democracy: as captive hostages, they have helped to provoke this situation by showing themselves incapable of halting the crime. For example, the role of governments, political parties, trade unions and the media in a future liberation seems indisputable, but for them to play their part, their work (that is, their practice) must be consistent with what we expect from these institutions. At least in theory, parties and unions could or perhaps should be the negotiators in the liberation process. As for the media, the hope is that they will be the bulwarks of transparency charged with uncovering everything that happens behind the scenes. If the future praxis of these institutions were consistent with these expectations, the role assigned to them in our kidnapping metaphor would be very different: they would cast off the role of hostages or accomplices to become negotiators working to liberate democracy.

Growing citizen disaffection, now reaching new heights, can be a huge incentive for basic structures of the democratic system to rethink their current modus operandi. If this disillusionment with the institutions continues to grow, we might ask whether the future of those institutions would be jeopardized. Whether for this or other reasons, there have been some notable examples of political actors attempting to revitalize their policies and their internal dynamics in recent years.

The Portuguese government is a case in point. Usually referred to in the press as the 'Portuguese miracle', it is an example of a coalition of left-wing parties governing together to achieve great economic success (reducing unemployment from 17.3 percent in 2013 to 8.6 percent in 2017, with economic growth above 2.5 percent of GDP) with policies that challenge the austerity model. This government, led by Prime Minister Antonio Costa and Minister of Finance Mario Centeno, has promoted social measures and reversed many long-standing policies, such as cuts in public salaries and pensions. Other measures introduced include reducing the VAT rate, halting privatization of key transport sectors and raising the minimum wage. Initially greeted with extreme distrust by representatives of European institutions, the coalition has now won their respect, to the point that in 2017, Mario Centeno was named president of the Eurogroup, replacing Jeroen Dijsselbloem. [1] This case seems to provide clear evidence that even during the current hijacking of democracy there is hope that political actors can take the initiative and regain their freedom and decision-making capacity.

While Portugal offers an example of a government's success in implementing policies that eschew the austerity line, other governments have also achieved recognition for developing and transforming channels of citizen participation. Today, several democratic experiments have been put in place by administrations seeking to involve citizens in politics and restore trust in representative institutions. One highly successful example is that of the 2013 Irish Constitutional Convention, a parliamentary initiative launched to discuss key points of constitutional reform. This pro-

---

1. Dijsselbloem had made some controversial statements, such as his observation in March 2017 that 'during the crisis of the euro, the countries of the North have shown solidarity with the countries affected by the crisis. As a Social Democrat, I attribute exceptional importance to solidarity. [But] you also have obligations. You cannot spend all the money on drinks and women and then ask for help. This principle applies at the personal, local, national and even European level'.

cess introduced random selection based on representative criteria such as socioeconomic status, age and gender to choose the members of the convention. A majority of the representatives, sixty-six of the total ninety-nine members, were chosen from the general population (not political representatives) in an attempt to represent a wide plurality of voices and concerns. The debates, which were live streamed on the internet, were held over the course of a year; their conclusions were taken both to Parliament and to the entire population for those measures that required approval through a referendum vote.

The use of random selection for political regeneration is a gamble that can pay off when it is used as a mechanism to incorporate representatives from a wider range of groups. This time-limited ad hoc process guarantees members' independence from pressure groups and introduces representatives who are not driven by their reelection prospects. The random selection method has been applied by institutions in other areas, as in the cases of citizen assemblies constituted in British Columbia and Ontario (Canada) to discuss possible voting law reforms, and by civil society, as in the renowned G1000 initiative in Belgium, introduced in 2011,[2] which sought to bring together one thousand randomly chosen citizens to deliberate on issues of public interest (van Reybrouck 2016).

In the field of political parties, other recent experiences have explored ways of breaking with traditional dynamics (or at least give the appearance of doing so). The current crisis of legitimacy and disaffection with institutions has had a singular effect on political parties, with a significant impact on social democratic platforms, which has perhaps spurred them to develop new strategies. Several political figures have recently emerged who present alternatives either in their traditional political agendas or in their understanding of the internal democracy of political platforms. One prominent example is Jeremy Corbyn, who was elected leader of the British Labour Party in 2015 as a result of grassroots

---

2.   This initiative was carried out during a period in which there was a clear crisis of governance in Belgium, which had been without a government for 540 days.

support rather than from the party's elites. Corbyn's rise to leadership has been accompanied by a significant increase in the number of party members, a phenomenon that challenges the trend in today's context. Another striking political figure is that of Bernie Sanders, who in 2015 announced his presidential candidacy for the Democratic Party in the United States. In his presentation, Sanders's message echoed the thesis of kidnapping, pointing out that in today's politics billionaires are the real owners of the political process because 'they can literally buy elections and candidates'.[3] In coherence with his concern, Sanders renounced 'super PAC' funding, the system through which candidates raise unlimited funds from large companies and wealthy individuals, thus putting the issue of campaign finance firmly on the agenda.

There have been other cases of new political parties forming as a rejection of traditional platforms and their internal dynamics. In Spain, multiple political platforms have either grown out of activist movements or are closely related to them in an attempt to consolidate alternative party models. These include municipal platforms that emerged in 2015, such as Barcelona en Comú, Ahora Madrid, Zaragoza en Común, Cádiz sí se puede, and many more that aspired to reconnect with the electorate and negotiate on behalf of interests that were not hijacked by other external economic forces.

While I am not arguing that Corbyn, Sanders or any another leader or political platform alone can liberate democracy from the oligarchies described in this book, I do believe it is useful to examine cases that have at least introduced – with varying degrees of success – questions of internal party democracy, sources of party funding and mechanisms to open up communication channels with civil society.

In general, the discourse of many parties and governments of very different ideologies is increasingly calling for greater transparency and participation (internal and external), and is defending the need to reconnect with citizens and put the lobbyists in their

---

3. The most significant moments of Sanders's presentation were reported in the press by Kane and Rucker (2015).

place. In all likelihood, the number of governments and political parties that take the initiative (and reclaim their freedom) to consolidate open two-way dialogue with citizens will have to grow before democracy can be released from its current captivity. These changes must be more than just platitudes that go no further than press releases or promising discourses; they must be fully incorporated into both the internal dynamics of the platforms and their political culture. By doing so, perhaps political parties and governments will return to their role as negotiators that they seem to have gradually abandoned.

EXPOSE THE SITUATION: A NECESSARY FIRST STEP

Despite the important transformations in the political realm described above, we must surely agree that as a society we cannot keep waiting for governments and political parties to take up the initiative on their own. Indeed, these actors may be in need of motivation from society. Several models of democracy now place their hope in strategies that develop what they call counterpowers (Rosanvallon 2008; Keane 2009 and 2013). These proposals hold that representative democracy must be complemented – not offset – by other participation mechanisms that can act as a counterweight to political and economic centres of power so as to ensure the plurality and redistribution of power across different spheres (Feenstra et al. 2017).

Among the proposals that are consistent with these models is John Keane's monitory democracy model, presented in 2009 in his work *The Life and Death of Democracy*. This proposal focuses on the democratizing effect that is hidden behind monitoring, that is, behind the control processes of political and economic power centres. Central to the monitory democracy model are the citizens and investigative journalists who play active roles in consolidating a series of counterpowers that examine relations and centres of power and publicly denounce cases of arbitrary decision making or abuse. In this way, sounding the alarm about kidnapping and revealing the identity, process and strategies of the kidnappers could become vital resources to defend democracy. Monitory democracy is not just an ideal to aspire to, but is inspired by numerous examples in which this process occurs and in which both society and the media uncover the kidnappers' plots, tricks and traps. Indeed, the current opaque behind-the-scenes processes of policy development are being challenged by a growing group of watchdogs dedicated to their exposure.

A striking case of denunciation and leaked information is that known as the Panama Papers. These documents were published in 2016 following a leak by an anonymous source (under the pseudonym of John Doe) and the collaboration of the newspaper that agreed to disclose them, the *Süddeustche Zeitung*, and the International Consortium of Investigative Journalists (in which more than 350 journalists from various countries participated). This case informed the international public about the network of tax havens used by twelve heads of state or prime ministers and more than 120 politicians, members of the business community, banks, actors, and top athletes and sportspersons. The investigation into these documents, which lasted for more than a year, disclosed the details of operations of dubious morality carried out by important personalities with the help of the law firm Mossack Fonseca and revealed, among many other things, the instruments used to favour corruption and tax evasion. An anonymous whistleblower and the journalistic endeavours of numerous media outlets have brought this type of information to public attention and exposed those responsible.[4]

Other recent cases have examined tax havens or uncovered the strategies employed by fraudsters and tax evaders. The so-called

---

4.   In this case, more than a hundred media outlets from a large number of countries collaborated. The media include the German outlets *Süddeustche Zeitung* (received information from John Doe), *Norddeutscher Rundfunk* and *Westdeutscher Rundfunk*; the British media *BBC* and *The Guardian*; the Argentinian newspaper *La Nación*; the Spanish media *la Sexta* and *El Confidencial*; the Swiss media *Sonntags Zeitung*; and many others.

Falciani list, for example, revealed the identity of 130,000 possible tax evaders following a leak by Hervé Falciani, an Italian-French systems engineer who had previously worked for the Swiss bank HSBC. The information it gathered uncovered the murky activities of the HSBC banking system in Switzerland and the methods used both to conceal goods and evade taxes for clients from the business world, as well as for politicians and athletes, and to launder money for warlords and arms and drug dealers.[5] Both the Panama Papers and the Falciani list uncovered shady banking procedures and the role of tax havens, key structures for those who act as kidnappers of democracy.

In addition to these well-known processes of control and monitoring of power, other examples of wrongdoing or abuse include the information uncovered by the WikiLeaks platform concerning highly sensitive details about the wars in Afghanistan and Iraq (among other issues) or the Snowden case in which former CIA technologist Edward Snowden, with the collaboration of *The Guardian* and the *Washington Post*, exposed the use of surveillance and espionage systems against millions of people worldwide.

Thus, although large sections of the mass media have been hijacked (as we saw in chapter 3), there are positive cases of resistance and dedication to building a critical and independent journalism. The proliferation of leaked information, anonymous whistleblowing platforms, civil groups demanding transparency, and international consortia of diligent journalists are combining to disclose the details of how power is exercised behind the scenes. The identities and strategies of the kidnappers of democracy are gradually being exposed, enabling the public to grasp a better understanding of the situation. While there is no doubt that this information can increase disaffection with and detachment from certain institutions or specific actors, it is also clear that the public exposure of abuses of power has become a significant way of curbing the captors' ability to act and disarming their offerings and

---

5. In February 2015, 140 journalists from 45 countries participated jointly in the publication of the list.

their seductive manipulations and strategies. Monitoring can play a major role in exposing them and threatening their power. It might also encourage their hostages, especially those working with them, to at least try to change their situation.

MASS CIVIL SOCIETY MOBILIZATION: OUR FINAL HOPE?

Monitoring the centres of power and restoring the freedom of democratic institutions may be two fundamental strategies in achieving our objective. However, we must also ask how citizens themselves can respond to this situation of captivity, the consequences of which they suffer first hand. It is ordinary members of the public that demonstrate, vote and consume, and for those reasons, it is important to ask if our actions might be decisive in the liberation of democracy.

Democratic models aiming to go beyond the representative model, whether deliberative or participatory, have for years reflected on the possible tools or democratic processes that could be incorporated into the political process to expand citizens' capacity to influence. This reflection has gained weight as a concept of civil society which, while polysemous and complex, is defined by Habermas as a 'non-governmental and non-economic associative storyline' whose purpose is to put pressure on the political system 'by way of siege', not with the intention to conquer (1996, 487). In other words, Habermas understands civil society as a sphere that does not hanker after political power, but rather as a space that, through peaceful means, maintains a constant influence on decision makers. Indeed, representatives' willingness to listen combined with citizens' active involvement would lead to a consolidated corrective dynamic in the political process and a healthy strong democracy.

For the purposes of our story, however, we must ask what civil society and citizens can do to liberate democracy from captivity. The answers involve diverse perspectives and proposals. Some proposals, for example, take the opposite line to Habermas by advocating that citizens should not rule out the idea of taking power (Žižek 2010). They urge the creation of new political parties capable of seizing power and, once in positions of responsibility, reversing established tendencies. Other proposals have less faith in this way forward, arguing that it will always be incomplete or frustrating because sooner or later these new platforms will not only capitulate to the classical dynamics of the traditional parties (and the iron law of the oligarchy described by Michels, chapter 2) but will also be unable to implement new policies, even if they achieve a significant share of power. The base of their argument is that rather than taking power, it is more important to create spaces of resistance and counterpower within broad spaces of self-organization promoted by and from society (Holloway 2002, Grae-ber 2013).

Beyond the key fundamental theoretical debates on this issue, other alternatives seem to have been taken up by those sections of civil society that are beginning to experiment with ways to curb the excessive power of the kidnappers of democracy. Alongside the monitoring of power centres described earlier, other dynamics or resources are available, such as resistance and pressure through strike action. At a time of austerity and cuts, strike action can be a valuable strategy, although it depends on whether trade unions are able to claw back some of their weight and capacity to influence. Demonstrations are another essential form of mass mobilization. Indeed, this strategy has spread worldwide in recent years with the so-called prodemocracy movements, referred to previously, such as the Pots and Pans revolution in Iceland (2008), the Arab Spring, the 15-M and Occupy movements (2011), # YoSoy132 in Mexico (2012), the Gezi Park protests in Turkey (2013), the Um-brella revolution in Hong Kong (2014), and la Nuit Debout (2016) and the Gilets Jaunes in France (2018). While all of these protests have their own distinctive style, they reveal the need for debate on the ideal conditions necessary for a healthy democracy and the role played by various centres of powers in setting it adrift. All these actions have involved a high level of mass mobilization and awareness, and in cases such as the movement in Iceland, have had far-reaching consequences that redefined the political process and brought corrupt representatives before the courts (Castells 2012). Such mobilizations have been widely imitated and in general have revived debates in the public sphere that could prove essential for the future of democracy. In short, they epitomize the dynamics of pressure (as in peaceful siege) exercised by civil society and put into practice the theories of authors such as Habermas.

Under the broad umbrella of mass mobilizations, a series of actions have clearly expressed society's anger about the current state of democracy and certain injustices. The *acampadas* (i.e., the permanent occupation of public spaces) witnessed in numerous contexts are highly symbolic political actions that seek to (re)introduce the debate on the meaning of ideal democracy. In addition, acts of civil disobedience – actions that violate legal norms through a previously notified organized but peaceful protest – have been effectively used, for example, by civil society action groups to prevent people in financial distress from being evicted from their homes through court orders instigated by the banks. During the crisis period, these same banks received public money to help with their financial problems. The human shields organized in Spain by PAH activists in front of these properties are a notable example of this resistance to the authorities and became a powerful gesture of struggle against inequality and injustice, which has not only stopped hundreds of evictions but has also been replicated in other places (including countries in much less unfavourable economic situations).

The crisis and economic difficulties have also driven the spread of citizen self-organization and self-management strategies into new areas; indeed, if this trend continues to grow, they have the potential to influence the power of large corporations. The proliferation of economic projects based on alternative and ethical principles now appears to be firmly established. In addition, initiatives such as time banks, which foster personal relationships mediated not by money but by skills and where each person contributes what they can in their free time, are springing up in many places and offer alternative social models of relating to each other.

Similar economic initiatives offer citizens other channels through which they can bring about change. One way of exerting pressure that is on the rise in some sections of the population is ethical consumption (Micheletti and Stolle 2015, Micheletti 2003, Cortina 2002). Advocates of responsible consumption understand that every purchase decision has social and political implications, and that they must weigh each seemingly insignificant, everyday consumer purchase. When we buy a product or service, not only do we acquire the good or service, but we also legitimize or encourage certain production policies; consciously or not, we are promoting and supporting, albeit indirectly, the company behind the product. As a result, a growing number of people are gathering information about the policies of goods and services providers in order to ensure their money and support go to companies with proven ethical responsibility (in matters of environmental protection, employment and workers' rights, transparency and consumer rights). They strive to avoid irresponsible companies that have unfair contract terms or a poor environmental record, exploit their workers, invest in tax havens, or flout political party funding regulations, among other unethical behaviours. This responsible consumption is limited in its effect as it is dependent on individuals' resources and requires widespread mobilization of responsible consumers to have any real or convincing practical impact. However, it is also true that because of the economic sector's key role in the kidnapping of democracy, responsible consumption could help to reduce the hijackers' power, or at least curb their growth. It should not be forgotten that the large multinationals and banks holding democracy ransom rely heavily on continued consumption of their products and services, which empowers citizens to abandon them in favour of more ethical alternatives. If only a few people do so the effect will be limited, but what if a large majority were to act?

In short, curbing the kidnappers' growing power also depends on citizens using all the tools and resources available to them.

These resources range from the way they self-organize, consume and vote, to demonstrations, strikes and civil disobedience. These individual and collective strategies, combined with the public exposure of power abuse by the captors and the urgent need for more cases of resistance by the kidnapped institutions themselves, may mean that the progressive dismantling of the hijacking is not just a pipe dream. What is certain is that Western democracies are living through tumultuous and complex times and if they do not take their current status seriously the outcome could be fatal, as in so many other kidnappings. The need to come up with liberation strategies, and more important, put them into practice and roll them out on a massive scale is a matter of great urgency.

REFERENCES

Alonso, Luis Enrique, and Carlos Jesús Fernández-Rodríguez. 2018. *Poder y sacrificio. Los nuevos discursos de la empresa* [*Power and sacrifice. The new discourses of the company*]. Madrid: Siglo XXI.

Alonso, Luis Enrique, Carlos J. Fernández Rodríguez and Rafael Ibáñez Rojo. 2017. "'I Think the Middle Class Is Disappearing'": Crisis Perceptions and Consumption Patterns in Spain'. *International Journal of Consumer Studies* 4(4): 389–96.

Alonso, Sonia. 2014. 'Votas pero no eliges: la democracia y la crisis de la deuda soberana en la eurozona [You vote but do not choose: Democracy and the sovereign debt crisis in the Eurozone]'. *Recerca. Revista de Pensament i Anàlisi* 15: 21–53.

Ayllón, Manuel. 1997. *Democracia Secuestrada*[*Kidnapped democracy*]. Madrid: Akal.

Barber, Benjamin. 2003. *Strong Democracy: Participatory Politics for a New Age*. Berkeley: University of California Press.

Bernaciak, Magdalena, Rebecca Gumbrell-McCormick, and Richard Hyman. 2014. *European Trade Unionism: From Crisis to Renewal?* Brussels: ETUI.

Betancourt, Ingrid. 2010. *Even Silence Has an End: My Six Years of Captivity in the Colombian Jungle*. New York: Penguin.

Boggs, Carl. 2001. *The End of Politics: Corporate Power and the Decline of the Public Sphere*. New York: Guilford Press.

Brooks, David. 2003 (January). 'The Triumph of Hope over Self-Interest'. *New York Times*. Retrieved from http://www.nytimes.com/2003/01/12/opinion/the-triumph-of-hope-over-self-interest.html (accessed 7 February 2018).

Castells, Manuel. 2012. *Networks of Outrage and Hope: Social Movements in the Internet Age*. Malden, MA: Polity.

Caul, Miki L., and Mark Gray. 2002. 'From Platform Declarations to Policy Outcomes: Changing Party Profiles and Partisan Influence over Policy'. In *Parties without Partisans: Political Change in Advanced Industrial Democracies*, edited by Russell Dalton and Martin Wattenberg. Oxford: Oxford University Press, 208–37.

Clark, Andrew. 2007. 'I Should Pay More Tax, Says US Billionaire Warren Buffet'. *The Guardian*. Retrieved from https://www.theguardian.com/business/2007/oct/31/usnews (accessed 10 July 2017).

Conill Sancho, Jesús. 2006. *Ética hermenéutica. Crítica desde la facticidad* [*Hermeneutical ethics. Criticism from the facticity*]. Madrid: Tecnos.

Cortina, Adela. 2002. *Por una ética del consumo* [*For an ethics of consumption*]. Madrid: Taurus.

Crouch, Colin. 2004. *Post-Democracy*. Cambridge: Polity.

———. 2011. *The Strange Non-Death of Neoliberalism*. Cambridge: Polity.

Culpepper, Pepper D., and Aidan Regan. 2014. 'Why Don't Governments Need Trade Unions Anymore? The Death of Social Pacts in Ireland and Italy'. *Socio-Economic Review* 12(4): 723–45.

Dahl, Robert A. 1989. *Democracy and Its Critics*. New Haven, CT: Yale University Press.

———. 2008. *On Democracy*. New Haven, CT: Yale University Press.

Dalton, Russell J., and Martin P. Wattenberg, eds. 2002. *Parties without Partisans: Political Change in Advanced Industrial Democracies*. Oxford: Oxford University Press.

Dardot, Pierre, and Christian Laval. 2019. *Never Ending Nightmare: How Neoliberalism Dismantles Democracy*. London: Verso Books. Kindle Edition.

Della Porta, Donatella. 2013. *Can Democracy Be Saved? Participation, Deliberation and Social Movements*. Cambridge: Polity.

DIAOQU. 2010 (October). 'Gary Noesner, el negociador de secuestros [Gary Noesner, the negotiator of kidnappings]'. *El Tiempo*. Retrieved from http://www.eltiempo.com/archivo/documento/MAM-4206695 (accessed 15 May 2017).

Eurobarometer. 2016 (Autumn). *National Report 86. Public Opinion in the European Union*. Retrieved from https://ec.europa.eu/spain/sites/spain/files/eurobarometro86-esp.pdf (accessed 17 November 2017).

Feenstra, Ramón A., Simon Tormey, Andreu Casero-Ripollés and John Keane. 2017. *Refiguring Democracy: The Spanish Political Laboratory*. London: Routledge.

Fishkin, James S. 2011. *When the People Speak: Deliberative Democracy and Public Consultation*. Oxford: Oxford University Press.

Flesher Fominaya, Cristina. 2014. *Social Movements and Globalizations. How Protest, Occupations and Uprising Are Changing the World*. New York: Palgrave.

Flew, Terry. 2007. *Understanding Global Media*. Basingstoke: Palgrave Macmillan.

Frank, Knight. 2017. *Global Wealth Report 2017: Where Are We Ten Years after the Crisis?* Retrieved from https://www.credit-suisse.com/corporate/en/articles/news-and-expertise/global-wealth-report-2017–201711.html (accessed 10 July 2018).

Fuentes-Nieva, Ricardo, and Nicholas Galasso. 2014. *Working for the Few: Political Capture and Economic Inequality 2014*. Oxfam International. Retrieved from https://www.oxfamintermon.org/sites/default/files/documentos/files/bp-working-for-few-political-capture-economic-inequality-200114-es.pdf (accessed 10 July 2018).

Galli, Carlo. 2013. *El malestar de la democracia* [*The unrest of democracy*]. México: Fondo de Cultura Económica.

Ganuza, Ernesto, and Joan Font. 2018. *¿Por qué la gente odia la política? Cómo nos gustaría que se tomaran las decisiones políticas?* [*Why do people hate politics? How would we like political decisions to be made?*]. Madrid: Los Libros de la Catarata.

García Márquez, Gabriel. 1999. *Noticia de un secuestro* [*News of a kidnapping*]. Barcelona: Nueva Narrativa.

García Marzá, Domingo. 1993. *Teoría de la democracia* [*Theory of democracy*]. Valencia: Nau.

González Esteban, Elsa, ed. 2013. *Ética y gobernanza: un cosmopolitismo para el siglo XXI* [*Ethics and governance: a cosmopolitanism for the 21st century*]. Granada: Comares.

Graeber, David. 2013. *The Democracy Project. A History. A Crisis. A Movement.* New York: Penguin.

Gray, Mark, and Miki Caul. 2000. 'Declining Voter Turnout in Advanced Industrial Democracies, 1950 to 1997: The Effects of Declining Group Mobilization'. *Comparative Political Studies* 33(9): 1091–122.

Habermas, J. 1996. *Between Facts and Norms. Contributions to a Discourse Theory of Law and Democracy.* Cambridge, MA: MIT Press.

Hardoon, Deborah. 2015. *Wealth: Having It All and Wanting More.* Oxfam International. Retrieved from https://www-cdn.oxfam.org/s3fs-public/file_attachments/ib-wealth-having-all-wanting-more-190115-en.pdf (accessed 10 July 2017).

Hardoon, Deborah, Ricardo Fuentes-Nieva and Sophia Ayele. 2016. *An Economy for the 1 Percent: How Privilege and Power in the Economy Drive Extreme Inequality And How This Can Be Stopped.* Oxfam International. Retrieved from https://www-cdn.oxfam.org/s3fs-public/file_attachments/bp210-economy-one-percent-tax-havens-180116-en_0.pdf (accessed 10 July 2018).

Herman, Edward S., and Robert Waterman McChesney. 1997. *The Global Media: The New Missionaries of Corporate Capitalism.* London: Burns and Oates.

Holloway, John. 2002. *Change the World Without Taking Power: The Meaning of Revolution Today.* London: Pluto Press.

Huber, Evelyne, and John D. Stephens. 2001. *Development and Crisis of the Welfare State: Parties and Policies in Global Markets.* Chicago: University of Chicago Press.

Isidore, Chris. 2013. 'Buffett Says He's Still Paying Lower Tax Rate Than His Secretary'. *CNN Business.* Retrieved from https://money.cnn.com/2013/03/04/news/economy/buffett-secretary-taxes/index.html (accessed 10 July 2017).

Johnson, Simon. 2009. 'The Quiet Coup'. *The Atlantic.* Retrieved from https://www.theatlantic.com/magazine/archive/2009/05/the-quiet-coup/307364/ (accessed 12 July 2017).

Jost, John T., and Aaron C. Kay. 2005. 'Exposure to Benevolent Sexism and Complementary Gender Stereotypes: Consequences for Specific and Diffuse Forms of System Justification'. *Journal of Personality and Social Psychology* 88: 498–509.

Jost, John T., Mahzarin R. Banaji and Brian A. Nosek. 2004. 'A Decade of System Justification Theory: Accumulated Evidence of Conscious and Unconscious Bolstering of the Status Quo'. *Political Psychology* 25(6): 881–919.

Jost, John T., Brett W. Pelham, Oliver Sheldon and Bilian Ni Sullivan. 2003. 'Social Inequality and the Reduction of Ideological Dissonance on Behalf of the System: Evidence of Enhanced System Justification among the Disadvantaged'. *European Journal of Social Psychology* 33(1): 13–36.

Kane, Paul, and Philip Rucker. 2015 (April). 'An Unlikely Contender: Sanders Takes On "Billionaire Class" in 2016 Bid'. *Washington Post.* Retrieved from https://www.washingtonpost.com/politics/sanders-takes-on-billionaire-class-in-launching-2016-bid-against-clinton/2015/04/30/4849fe32-ef3a-11e4-a55f-38924fca94f9_story.html? Utm_term =.f9300f8b0082 (accessed 7 March 2018).

Keane, John. 2009. *The Life and Death of Democracy.* London: Simon & Schuster.

———. 2013. *Democracy and Media Decadence.* Cambridge: Cambridge University Press.

Klein, Naomi. 2007. *The Shock Doctrine: The Rise of Disaster Capitalism.* New York: Macmillan.

Kocka, Jürgen. 2016. *Capitalism: A Short History.* Princeton, NJ: Princeton University Press.

Kovach, Bill, and Tom Rosenstiel. 2007. *The Elements of Journalism: What Newspeople Should Know and the Public Should Expect.* New York: Three Rivers Press.

Lakoff, George. 2014. *The All New Don't Think of an Elephant! Know Your Values and Frame the Debate.* White River Junction, VT: Chelsea Green Publishing.

Lane, Robert E. 2004. 'The Fear of Equality'. In *Political Psychology: Key Readings*, edited by John T. Jost and Jim Sidanius. New York: Taylor & Francis.

Llorens, Marc, and Maria Moreno. 2008. *El secuestro en Latinoamérica: Los ojos de la víctima [Kidnapping in Latin America: In the eyes of the victim]*. Creative Commons. Retrieved from https://losojosdelavictima.wordpress.com/leer-el-libro/ (accessed 3 April 2018).

Mair, Peter. 2005. 'Democracy Beyond Parties'. Paper presented at the Center for the Study of Democracy, University of California, Irvine. Retrieved from https://escholarship.org/uc/item/3vs886v9 (accessed 20 March 2019.

———. 2013. *Ruling the Void: The Hollowing of Western Democracy*. London: Verso Trade.

McAllister, Ian. 2007. 'The Personalization of Politics'. In *The Oxford Handbook of Political Behavior*, edited by Russell Dalton and Hans-Dieter Klingemann. Oxford: Oxford University Press, 571–85.

McChesney, Robert W. 2015. *Rich Media, Poor Democracy: Communication Politics in Dubious Times*. New York: The New Press.

Micheletti, Michelle. 2003. *Political Virtue and Shopping: Individuals, Consumerism and Collective Action*. New York: Palgrave.

Micheletti, Michelle, and Dietlind Stolle. 2015. 'Consumer Strategies in Social Movements'. In *The Oxford Handbook of Social Movements*, edited by Donatella Della Porta and Mario Diani. Oxford: Oxford University Press, 478–93.

Michels, Robert. 2001. *Political Parties: A Sociological Study of the Oligarchical Tendencies of Modern Democracy*. Ontario: Batoche Books.

Montero, Luis Miguel. 2016. *El club de las puertas giratorias: De los escaños a la poltrona: Todos los privilegios de los políticos que pasan a la empresa privada— y viceversa [The revolving doors club: From the seats to the armchair, all the privileges of the politicians that pass to the private company—and vice versa]*. Madrid: La Esfera de los Libros.

Mora, Rosa. 2004 (April). 'Saramago critica los males de la democracia en *Ensayo sobre la Lucidez* [Saramago criticizes the evils of democracy in *Seeing*]'. *El País*. Retrieved from https://elpais.com/diario/2004/04/27/cultura/1083016804_850215.html (accessed 25 August 2017).

Morin, François. 2015. *L'Hydre Mondiale. L'Oligopole Bancaire [The world hydra, the bank oligopoly]*. Montreal: Lux Éditeur.

O'Donnell, María. 2016. *El secuestro de los Born [The Born kidnapping]*. Madrid: Debate.

Plataforma de Afectados por la Hipoteca (PAH). 2013 (May). 'De ciudadano a presidente [From citizen to president]'. Retrieved from http://escrache.afectadosporlahipoteca.com/2013/05/04/419/ (accessed 12 July 2017).

Piqueras, José Antonio, Antonio Laguna, Francesc A. Martinez and Antonio Alaminos. 2011. *El secuestro de la democracia. Corrupción y dominación política en la España actual [The kidnapping of democracy: Corruption and political domination in the present-day Spain]*. Madrid: Akal.

Rodrik, Dani. 2011. *The Globalization Paradox: Democracy and the Future of the World Economy*. W. W. Norton & Company.

Rosanvallon, Pierre. 2008. *Counter-Democracy: Politics in an Age of Distrust*. Cambridge: Cambridge University Press.

Rubiales, Francisco. 2005. *Democracia secuestrada [Kidnapped democracy]*. Córdoba: Almuzara.

Sánchez-Cuenca, Ignacio. 2014. *La impotencia democrática: Sobre la crisis política de España [Democratic impotence: On the political crisis in Spain]*. Madrid: Los Libros de la Catarata.

Sartori, Giovanni. 1989. 'Video-power'. *Government and Opposition* 24(1): 39–53.

————. 2009. *La democracia en 30 lecciones* [*Democracy in 30 lessons*]. Madrid: Taurus.

Scharpf, Fritz W. 2000. 'Economic Changes, Vulnerabilities, and Institutional Capabilities'. In *Welfare and Work in the Open Economy*, edited by Fritz W. Scharpf and Vivien A. Schimdt. Oxford: Oxford University Press, 21–124.

Schumpeter, Joseph A. 2003. *Capitalism, Socialism and Democracy*. London: Routledge.

La Sexta Noche. 2017. 'José Mujica: "Vivimos en una democracia secuestrada" [We live in a kidnapped democracy]'. Retrieved from http://www.lasexta.com/programas/sexta-noche/entrevistas/jose-mujica-vivimos-en-una-democracia-secuestrada-que-es-mucho-peor-que-una-dictadura-evi-dente_2016120358433f220cf245500ad1e822.html (accessed 24 March 2019).

Sinova, Justino, and Javier Tusell. 1990. *El secuestro de la democracia. Cómo regenerar el sistema político español* [*The kidnapping of democracy: How to revive the Spanish political system*]. Barcelona: Plaza and Janés.

Smith, Adam. 2007. *Inquiry into the Nature and Causes of the Wealth of Nations*. New York: MetaLibri Digital Library. Originally published in 1776.

Stiglitz, Joseph E. 2008 (July). 'The End of Neoliberalism?' *Economist's View*. Retrieved from https://economistsview.typepad.com/economistsview/2008/07/stiglitz-the-en.html (accessed 5 November 2017).

Streeck, Wolfgang. 2011. 'The Crises of Democratic Capitalism'. *New Left Review* 71, 5–29.

Tormey, Simon. 2015. *The End of Representative Politics*. Cambridge: Polity.

UNDOC. 2006. *Counter-Kidnapping Manual*. Vienna: United Nations Office on Drugs and Crime.

Upchurch, Martin, Graham Taylor, and Andy Mathers. 2009. 'The Crisis of "Social Democratic" Unionism: The "Opening Up" of Civil Society and the Prospects for Union Renewal in the United Kingdom, France, and Germany'. *Labor Studies Journal* 34(4): 519–42.

Varoufakis, Yanis. 2015. 'Our Athens Spring'. *Mediapart*. Retrieved from https://blogs.mediapart.fr/edition/les-invites-de-mediapart/article/250815/our-athens-spring.

————. 2016 (February). 'The EU No Longer Serves the People – Democracy Demands a New Beginning', *The Guardian*. Retrieved from https://www.theguardian.com/commentisfree/2016/feb/05/eu-no-longer-serves-people-europe-diem25 (accessed 8 August 2017).

Van Reybrouck, David. 2016. *Against Elections: The Case for Democracy*. London: Random House.

Welp, Yanina. 2018. *Todo lo que necesitas saber sobre la democracia del siglo XXI* [*Everything you need to know about 21st century democracy*]. Barcelona: Paidós.

Wolf, Martin. 2016 (January). 'The Economic Losers Are in Revolt Against the Elites'. *Financial Times*. Retrieved from https://www.ft.com/content/135385ca-c399–11e5–808f-8231cd71622e (accessed 18 September 2017).

Zinn, Howard. 1968. *Disobedience and Democracy: Nine Fallacies on Law and Order*, vol. 4. New York: South End Press.

Žižek, Slavoj. 2010. 'From Democracy to Divine Violence'. In *Democracy in What State?*, edited by Giorgio Agamben, 100–119. New York: Columbia University Press.

INDEX

ABOUT THE AUTHOR

Ramón A. Feenstra teaches in the Department of Philosophy and Sociology at the Universitat Jaume I of Castellón (Spain). He holds bachelor's degrees in advertising and public relations (2005) and history (2013), and a PhD in moral philosophy (2010). His research interests include democracy theory and communication ethics and he is the author of *Refiguring Democracy: Spanish Political Laboratory* (2017), *Democracia monitorizada en la era de la nueva galaxia mediática* [Monetary democracy in the new media galaxy era] (2012), and numerous articles in journals such as *The International Journal of Press/Politics, Media International Australia, Voluntas, The Journal of Civil Society* and *Policy Studies.* He is currently chief editor of the journal *Recerca* and member of the research project 'Applied Ethics and Open Government' (UJI-A2016-04) funded by the Universitat Jaume I de Castellón.